Living in Love

Living in Love

Book One in the series
THE FRUIT OF THE SPIRIT:
THE PRODUCE OF GOD'S PRESENCE

by
SUSAN SLADE
and
SUSIE HALE

Wyatt House Publishing
Mobile, Alabama

Wyatt House books may be ordered through booksellers or by contacting:

WYATT HOUSE PUBLISHING
399 Lakeview Dr. W.
Mobile, Alabama 36695
www.wyattpublishing.com

Because of the dynamic nature of the Internet, any web address or links contained in this book may have changed since publication and may no longer be valid.

Cover design by: Mark Wyatt
Interior design by: Mark Wyatt
ISBN 13:978-1-954798-16-8

Printed in the United States of America

DEDICATION

I dedicate this book to three godly men who Jesus has definitely given me as bonus family. T. Dorrell Hall, my first pastor who did not think it odd or unacceptable for a precocious preschooler to be in "big church" and ultimately interrupt his sermon to receive the Lord. He later was the first to sign my ordination certificate. He is now "coaching" Susie and me to continue maturing our walks with the Lord. He has become a bonus uncle to me. I refer to T. D.'s younger brother, Dudley Hall, as "Papa." He presided over my ordination service and has served as a father in the faith. These two brothers have consistently been living examples of the Father's love poured into my life. Now, through T.D., I have come to know his son, Dan Hall. Like me, Dan is a quadriplegic but still actively fulfilling his calling, serving as a pastor and speaker. God has given me a great love for this brother even though we have never met in person. His tenacity inspires me to persevere in my own service to the Lord and never ever give up!

Susan R. Slade

I dedicate this book to my co-author, Susan R. Slade. She loves me as much as any biological family member, and Jesus has truly made us sisters. She loves me when depression makes me less lovable. She has loved me through sorrowful times of losing a family member or dear friend. We have cried on each other's shoulders many times, but we truly spend more time laughing out loud and enjoying the home the Lord has graciously created for the two of us as a family.

Susie Hale

ACKNOWLEDGEMENTS

T.D. Hall – spiritual life coach, prayer partner, and encourager extraordinaire!

Richard Wayne Albin – photographer & AI assisted cover picture

David Jack – hairstylist for both Susan and Susie

Team Uplift – Dana Carr, Chelsea Landsee, Nick Shepard, Zach Sullivan who lift Susan into and out of her power chair but also lift us both up with their encouragement

PJM Board Members – Dana Carr, Dane Carr, Crystal Foster, Eric Little, Nick Miller

PJM Treasurer – Rick Ivey

Mark Wyatt of Wyatt House Publishing

Jennifer Staats – seamstress/designer/tailor of Miss Slade's clothing

Robert Young – special gift to cover publishing costs

PJM "Generous Gems" – those who give regularly to our ministry

If the Lord leads you to contribute to our ministry monetarily, you may do so via our website https://www.preciousjewelsministries.com by PayPal, credit card, or debit card. Or you can send funds via Venmo @Susan-PJM. You may also mail a check made out to Precious Jewels Ministries to P.O. Box 1343, Hurst, TX 76053.

Soli Deo Gloria!

FOREWORD

Susan and Susie are truly faithful servants. They are using what God has given them without reservation or complaint. They have used the circumstances of life as a platform to declare the tender and majestic glories of our God. As I read through some of the devotional thoughts, I felt like I was opening the doors to the rooms in a giant castle; rooms that I had some familiarity with, but there was something fresh and new in each room. Their observations on the various texts and insights into the fresh word of God enticed me to open another door, and another.

I have known Susan Slade since she was a young girl. We have discussed most of the issues of life, and I seldom find someone as interesting to talk with. She has never allowed obstacles to stop her. She simply faced them, committed them to God, and moved on. I am so glad she is in my corner as a prayer warrior. She knows how to fight the real battle with the real weapons.

I have known Susie Hale for several years and have always been inspired by her genuine spirit to serve. God made her for her calling, and she is faithful. I am truly grateful for her and her partnership with Susan. Together those girls make a formidable team. I am so honored to know them both.

Thank you, Susan and Susie, for graciously giving what you have. God is taking your bread and fish and feeding multitudes.

Dudley Hall, M.Div.
President, Kerygma Ventures
https://kerygmaventures.com/speaker/dudley-hall/

INTRODUCTION

For a few years we have wanted to write a series of devotionals focusing on The Fruit of the Spirit found in Galatians 5:22-23. *Living in Love* is the first book in the series called *The Fruit of the Spirit: The Produce of His Presence.* We have focused on scripture from the New Testament for this first book but hope at some point in the future to write devotionals on the use of "love" in the Old Testament. Quotations are numbered in parenthesis such as [1] and are identified on the NOTES page. From time to time, we use words or phrases unique to Susan which are defined on the page called DEFINITIONS OF "SUSANISMS." If you are reading this book and are not sure you belong to Jesus, go to JEWELS OF SALVATION in the back of the book.

Here are some ideas that may help you get the most out of this book.

1. Read one page per day as your "devotional" time. Pray about the last paragraph which we call the "challenge" and try to implement the suggestions.

2. Read it with your Bible open to the passage to see the context of the scripture quoted. You may want to take notes in the margins or in a notebook to use it as more of a Bible

Study. Write down your own insights from reading the passage.

3. Listen to or sing along with the suggested worship songs.

4. When it lends itself to it, say the scripture as a prayer personalizing it with your name or the name of a friend for whom you are interceding.

5. Look up more of the word meanings by going to www.blueletterbible.com to get the Strong's number. Perhaps use a good dictionary such as those listed in the bibliography. We really like Zodhiates.

6. Here are some of our favorite websites to help you in your own studies:

    a. www.biblegateway.com

    b. www.biblehub.com

    c. www.blueletterbible.com

    d. www.gotquestions.org

Chuck Swindoll gave his own definition of love in a great sermon we listen to here:
https://www.youtube.com/watch?v=MX-KH4EbqQF8&t=3286s

Listens

Overlooks

Values

Expresses

CONTENTS

LOVE DEFINITIONS

Here we are listing the basic definitions of the words used for love in both the Old and New Testaments. We have quoted these from (1)*The Complete Word Study Dictionary: Old Testament*, Warren Baker and Eugene Carpenter, eds. and (2)*The Complete Word Study Dictionary: New Testament,* Spiros Zodhiates, ed. Each entry continues on to show the different nuances of the words in specific verses. These two books are an excellent resource for your study library. The numbering system Corresponds to *Strong's Exhaustive Concordance of the Bible.* In each devotional post, we will label the words for love with the *Strong's* number for their definition. You can return to these pages to be reminded of the definition(s) of love for that passage.

H157 – `*āhaḇ* – a verb meaning to love. The semantic range of the verb includes loving or liking objects and things . . . The word also conveys love for other people, love for God, and also God's love of people.

H160 – `*ahᵃḇāh* – a feminine noun meaning love. The word often signifies a powerful, intimate love between a man and a woman, love between friends, God's love for His people. Frequently, it is associated with forming a covenant, which enjoins loyalty.

H2617 – *hesed* – A masculine noun indicating kindness, lovingkindness, mercy, goodness, faithfulness, love, acts

of kindness. This aspect of God is one of several important features of His character: truth; faithfulness; mercy;
steadfastness; justice; righteousness; goodness.

G25 – *agapáō* – To esteem, love, indicating a direction
of the will and finding one's joy in something or someone . . . Agapáō and never philéō is used of love toward
our enemies. The range of philéō is wider than of agapáō
which stands higher than philéō because of its moral import, i.e., love that expresses compassion. We are thus
commanded to love (agapáō) our enemies, to do what is
necessary to turn them to Christ, but never to befriend
them (philéō) by adopting their interests and becoming
friends on their level.

G26 – *agápē* – To love. Love, affectionate regard, good-
will, benevolence. With reference to God's love, it is
God's willful direction toward man. It involves God doing what He knows is best for man and not necessarily
what man desires.

G27 *agapētós* - . . . beloved of God, means chosen by
Him to salvation

G5360 – *philadelphía* – one who loves his brother.
Brotherly love. In the NT, used of love of Christians one
to another, brotherly love out of a common spiritual life

G5368 – *philéō* – Loved, dear, friend. To love. Generally . . . to have affection for someone. . . Believers are never told to love their enemies with the word philéō because that would mean to have the same interests as they have.

G5387 - *philóstorgos*; from G5384 and *storgé* (cherishing one's kindred, especially parents or children); fond of natural relatives, i.e. fraternal towards fellow Christians:—kindly affectioned.

FRUIT OF THE SPIRIT FLOWS FROM THE FOUNDATION OF LOVE

But the fruit of the Spirit is love[G26], joy, peace, patience, kindness, goodness, faithfulness, gentleness, and self-control. Against such things there is no law.

Galatians 5:22-23

I will give you a new heart and put a new spirit within you; I will remove your heart of stone and give you a heart of flesh. And I will put My Spirit within you and cause you to walk in My statutes and to carefully observe My ordinances.

Ezekiel 36:26-27

When I surrendered my life to Jesus,
He replaced my heart of stone,
a heart that could not obey Him
through any will of my own.
He placed a new Spirit in me,
my Comforter, and my Guide.
His presence is ever with me,
always walking by my side.
The Holy Spirit empowers me to
become more and more like Christ.

His power within me develops
certain characteristics in my life.
Love is the first in the list
and from it the other traits flow.
Love for God and love for neighbor
fulfills the Law, as we know.
Still, I must choose daily
to tap into the Spirit's power
If I am to demonstrate love
consistently, hour by hour.
Love, joy, peace, patience, kindness, goodness,
faithfulness,gentleness, self-control
Can only be fully developed
when the Holy Spirit freely flows.
Lord, help me be more like Jesus.
His image and fruit may I bear.
As people see His nature in me,
the Good News of Jesus I'll share.
May I begin each morning
by praying that I will submit
To the Holy Spirit's prompting
and purposely follow it.

PRIORITY NUMBER ONE:
LOVING JESUS

Anyone who loves[G5368] *his father or mother more than Me is not worthy of Me; anyone who loves*[G5368] *his son or daughter more than Me is not worthy of Me; and anyone who does not take up his cross and follow Me is not worthy of Me. Whoever finds his life will lose it, and whoever loses his life for My sake will find it.*

Matt. 10:37-39

> Loyal disciples sacrificially choose their essential priorities. . . Faithfulness to Christ calls for a commitment to Him that supersedes all other commitments.
> (3)

Priorities. We are being "coached" by a dynamic 92-year-young minister named T. D. Hall, and one of the first lessons he shared with us was the Five Priorities. They are: 1) God, 2) Family, 3) Relationships, 4) Health, 5) Career. If we get that first priority right, many other things will fall into place because they build on the foundation of a relationship with the Lord. However, there are times when placing Jesus first in our lives creates conflict in other areas. Those who come from non-believing families may have issues that arise in what should be our closest earthly relationships. They may be teased for being a "goody two-shoes" or worse, disowned or even threatened with death if their family is of another religion. As Swindoll explained in the quote above, we sometimes have to make sacrificial choices. After telling the early disciples that they needed to place Him above even their parents and children, Jesus went further to say they needed to "take up their cross" and follow Him. At this point in His ministry, the Twelve still did not understand that the Lord's ultimate goal was to die in our place on a cross; but they had all seen Roman crucifixions. They certainly understood it to be the most horrific way to die. Jesus made it clear that those who follow Him must be willing to sacrifice even to the point of death for Him. However, if we lose our lives (literally or even figuratively) because of our commitment to Christ, we will find that we have found a life worth far more than anything we lost.

Is our devotion to Jesus so passionate that we place Him above all other relationships and even our own lives? In today's immensely self-centered society, it may be hard to imagine denying oneself to "take up our cross." There are magazines on the store shelves titled *People*, *Us,* and *Self*. We are urged to engage in "self-care" which is not inherently wrong if it means taking care of priority number four which is health, emotional and physical. But if it means placing our own needs above all others to the exclusion of following what Christ has called us to do, then it becomes narcissism. In what ways do we demonstrate that our love and commitment to Jesus "supersedes all other commitments."

Father, help us to understand what it means to place You first in our lives. Then enable us to follow through on that commitment knowing that in You, we have abundant life.

NOT IN THE TOP TEN

*Just then a man came up to Jesus and inquired,
"Teacher, what good thing must I do to obtain eternal
life?""Why do you ask Me about what is good?" Jesus
replied. "There is only One who is good. If you want to
enter life, keep the commandments.""Which ones?" the
man asked. Jesus answered, "'Do not murder, do not
commit adultery, do not steal, do not bear false witness, honor your father and mother, and love^{G25} your
neighbor as yourself."'*

Matt. 19:16-19

W e may all recall this scene which ended with Jesus telling the young man to sell all he had and
give to the poor, at which point the man walked away
sad because he had great riches. Ultimately, he chose
his financial security over following Jesus. However, today let's focus on the list of commandments Jesus gave
the man. You may recognize most of them from the Ten
Commandments, but what about that last one: "love
your neighbor as yourself." That one is NOT in the top
ten. Or is it? It is commanded, just not in the list of commandments recorded in Exodus 20 and Deuteronomy 5.

> *Leviticus 19:18 Do not seek revenge or
> bear a grudge against any of your peo-
> ple, but love^{H157} your neighbor as your-
> self. I am the LORD.*

However, if you look closely at the Ten Commandments, there are four that describe our relationship to God, one regarding our relationship to our parents, and five that involve our relationship to others, i.e. our neighbors. If we "love our neighbors as ourselves," we are following the Golden Rule: "In everything, then, do to others as you would have them do to you. For this is the essence of the Law and the Prophets" (Matt. 7:12). If we treat others the way we would like them to treat us; we will not murder, commit adultery, steal, bear false witness, or covet what they have. Therefore, loving our neighbor as we love ourselves covers the last five of the Ten Commandments.

Perhaps we should ask ourselves daily, "How have I done today as far as loving my neighbor?" Notice that we are not to respond to them with how they may have treated us. We are to treat them the way we would like to be treated. Ask the Lord to infuse you with His love for others. Then demonstrate His love to them as He prompts you.

Father, please fill us to the brim with Your love to be able to love even those who do not love us in return.

LOVE: THE PROTOTYPE

Now one of the scribes had come up and heard their debate. Noticing how well Jesus had answered them, he asked Him, "Which commandment is the most important of all?"Jesus replied, "This is the most important:[G4413] *'Hear O Israel, the Lord our God, the Lord is One. Love*[G25] *the Lord your God with all your heart and with all your soul and with all your mind and with all your strength.' The second is this: 'Love*[G25] *your neighbor as yourself.' No other commandment is greater than these."*

Mark 12:28-31

> *Prōtos*[G4413] meaning "foremost (in time, place, order or importance):—before, beginning, best, chief(-est), first (of all), former" [4]

The commandment to "Love the Lord your God" is the prototype from which all other commands develop. We are to love God with all our emotional, mental, and physical abilities. Our love for God cannot be simply a mental assent or the "Love you, bye!" we tag onto the end of a phone call with a family member. This love is a complete outpouring emanating from the deepest part of us. Our love is not only heartfelt but results in action. In John 15:10, we learn that our love for the

Lord and desire to remain in His love, leads us to obeying God's commands. We demonstrate our love for God when we pour all our strength—our physical, mental, and moral abilities—into obeying what He has shown us in His word, the Bible. Following what is taught in scripture should be out of intrinsic devotion to our Father God rather than obligatory obedience. Our obedience derives from the refuge of our redemptive relationship with the Father whose love for us is perfect and cannot be matched by any earthly love.

Worship is one way we express our love to God. A great example of worshiping God in song is Babbie Mason's "With All My Heart." You can sing along with her here: https://www.youtube.com/watch?v=3CD8NOWuo-JU. Do not only express loving Him through song and prayer. Go forth from the time of loving worship to be His hands, feet, and voice demonstrating His love to others. In so doing, you are also confirming your love for the Lord by doing His will. Tomorrow, we will examine an example of how God wants us to love.

Father, we love You. May we remember to tell You we love You every day. Let our obedience to Your commands truly be an expression of our love and gratitude to You because You first loved us (1 John 4:19).

LOVE YOUR ENEMIES (EASIER SAID THAN DONE)

But to those of you who will listen, I say: Love[G25] your enemies, do good to those who hate you, bless those who curse you, pray for those who mistreat you. . . Do to others as you would have them do to you. If you love[G25] those who love[25] you, what credit is that to you? Even sinners love[G25] those who love[G25] them. . . But love[G25] your enemies, do good to them, and lend to them, expecting nothing in return. Then your reward will be great, and you will be sons of the Most High; for He is kind to the ungrateful and wicked. Be merciful, just as your Father is merciful.

Luke 6:27-28, 31-32, 35-36 (see also Matt. 5:43-47)

Part of us wishes the Lord had left this passage out of His sermon. It is one thing to say, "I choose to love my enemies," but another thing entirely to do good things for them. This seemingly impossible task is only possible as we are God's instruments of compassion in the hands of the Holy Spirit. By "pray for them," we do not think Jesus means to pray they go away and leave us alone. We should pray for God to draw them to Jesus and bless them as objects of His grace. We should pray that Jesus draws them into the transformative reality of salvation. When we see that type of prayer answered, our enemies become our brothers and sisters in the

Lord. Reading the stories at www.persecution.com is a humbling experience as so many of them express the desire to see the salvation of the very ones who persecuted them. "Do to others as you would have them do to you." This is the principle that we were taught as children called "The Golden Rule." Jewish rabbis and even other religions taught a similar concept but stated it negatively—Do _not_ do something to others that you would not want done to you. Jesus, however, elevated this and taught it in the affirmative. We are to do good things to and for others like we would want them to do for us because it is not only the right thing but commanded by Jesus. This is placed in the passage on doing good to our enemies which tells us we do not make an exception to the Golden Rule just because we do not think a person deserves to be treated well. We are to treat *everyone* like we would want to be treated. Jesus is saying, "Don't pat yourself on the back for returning love to someone who already loves you." The greater love is to emulate the love of Jesus who loved us unconditionally even while we were His enemies (Rom. 5:10). Jesus teaches that we are to do good for people even if they never have and probably never will return the favor. Generously and unconditionally loving our enemies is foolproof evidence that we truly are the children of God. In obeying these commands of Jesus, we are imitating His behavior because God gives generously to both believers and non-believers. For example, God provides sunlight and rain to grow crops for food not just for those who love Him but for all mankind.

You may not have an obvious enemy in the sense of someone who is persecuting you or at war against you. However, is there someone you cannot seem to forgive? Someone who has hurt you deeply? Pray for them. Ask the Lord to enable you to forgive and perhaps even show kindness to them. Forgive as He has forgiven you—unconditionally and completely even though you did not deserve it.

Father, may Your Spirit flow through us and enable us to love even our enemies.

NEVER NEGLECT JUSTICE AND LOVE

Woe to you Pharisees! You pay tithes of mint, rue, and every herb, but you disregard justice and the love[G26] of God. You should have practiced the latter without neglecting the former.

Luke 11:42

W hat did Jesus describe as more important than meticulously following the law and traditions? What are the most essential elements of following the Lord? Jesus emphasized "justice and the love of God." The Prophet Jeremiah quotes Father God as describing Himself as embodying these attributes.

> Jeremiah 9:23-24 (ESV): Thus says the Lord: "Let not the wise man boast in his wisdom, let not the mighty man boast in his might, let not the rich man boast in his riches, but let him who boasts boast in this, that he understands and knows me, that I am the Lord who practices steadfast love[H2617], justice, and righteousness in the earth. For in these things I delight, declares the Lord."

To exemplify the qualities of love, justice, and righteousness is to emulate the character of God. Justice and love being practiced by His children is what truly brings God great pleasure and brings glory to His Holy name. Jesus did not say that people would know we belong to Him by our attention to the details of the Law. He said, "By this everyone will know that you are My disciples, if you love[G26] one another" (John 13:35). Justice and Love—If you belong to Jesus, you are already filled with His Holy Spirit and are empowered to demonstrate justice and love.

Are you diligently exemplifying these Christlike qualities as you go about your day-to-day business? Are there ways you can improve in loving God and loving others? When confronted with a difficult situation, ask yourself what the loving response would be instead of reacting immediately. Take a breath, pray silently, and ask the Lord to infuse you with His love *before* responding because the only way we can truly love our neighbor is to have the love of Jesus overwhelmingly overflowing in our lives. Think of some specific ways to show love to others this week, write them down, and do them!

Father, we pray that Your Holy Spirit flowing through us demonstrates love and justice to others. May we grow to be more and more like Jesus in these two attributes.

GOD SO LOVED

For God so loved[G25] the world that He gave His one and only Son, that everyone who believes in Him shall not perish but have eternal life.

John 3:16

For God so greatly loved[G25] and dearly prized the world that He [even] gave up His only begotten (unique) Son, so that whoever believes in (trusts in, clings to, relies on) Him shall not perish (come to destruction, be lost) but have eternal (everlasting) life.

John 3:16 (AMPC)

The world in this instance means all kinds of people in the world, Jews and Gentiles, from all over the world, living under the fallen "world system." In other words, sinners of all kinds. Sin is anything that falls short of God's holiness, whether that is an overt evil act or the omission of performing the good we know to do (James 4:17). God gave His "only begotten Son." We as believers are *adopted* into God's family, but Jesus was actually God's Son born of the virgin Mary, conceived in her by the Holy Spirit. Believing in Jesus is much more than intellectually acknowledging His existence. It is a complete understanding that we must lean into, depend upon, Jesus for all that we are, all that we have, and all that we ever will be. It is a total surrender of our lives to

His care by faith that He is the only way to the Father, the only path to peace with God, the only entry way to spend eternity in the presence of the Lord.

> *John 14:6 Jesus answered, "I am the way and the truth and the life. No one comes to the Father except through Me."*

God loved us so much He "gave" His Son, Jesus, not only to walk among us on earth as a living portrait of that love, but to die in our place to redeem us from the wrath of God and save us from the punishment sinners deserve:

> *Rom. 3:23 For the wages of sin is death, but the gift of God is eternal life in Christ Jesus our Lord.*

Our redemption is a gift bestowed on us when we place our trust in Jesus. It is free to us and cannot be earned because we can never measure up to God's holiness. However, it was costly, the most expensive gift we will ever receive. Jesus died an excruciating death on the cross to purchase that gift for us. He was then raised from the grave to take His rightful place at the right hand of God. Those who believe—trust in Jesus—have eternal life. Death here on earth is simply the portal to enter the Lord's presence forever. If you have never surrendered your life to God by trusting in Jesus to redeem you from sin, there is a more detailed description of how to receive this gift in the back of this book.

Father, we pray for those who will read this book that they will be drawn closer to You through the power of Your Holy Spirit and faith in Jesus Christ.

NO GREATER LOVE

*This is My commandment, that you love^G25 one anoth-
er as I have loved^G25 you. Greater love^G26 has no one
than this, that he lay down his life for his friends.*

John 15:12-13

Jesus had told His disciples
He would call them servants no more.
He shared the Father's intent with them;
They were beloved friends He adored.
And then He explained the measure
Of His love for these intimate brothers
That He would willingly give His life
For them and so many others.
Jesus laid down His life for me,
A sinner He chose to befriend.
No greater love story has ever been known
Than the one Jesus lived and John penned.

KNOWN BY OUR LOVE

A new commandment I give you: Love[G25] one another. As I have loved[G25] you, so you also must love[G25] one another. By this everyone will know that you are My disciples, if you love[G26] one another.

John 13:34-35

How *did* Jesus love? Jesus loved with His words but also through corresponding actions to demonstrate His love. His love was our example. Jesus loved wholeheartedly and unconditionally. The disciples were sinners just like you and me, but Jesus loved them as His own brothers. At one point all we who believe were dead in our sin, but when the Lord drew us to Him and we trusted in Jesus, we died *to* our sin and were redeemed, re-created, and enveloped in His righteousness. Jesus loved so intensely that He willingly died an excruciating, demoralizing death on the cross for His people—all who trust in Him—both Jews and Gentiles. As Christ-followers, we are to love as He loved—sacrificially. We are enabled to love sacrificially when we trust in Jesus. We are only capable of this kind of love through the power of the Holy Spirit within us.

As believers, we are to be known by our love for each other. How will people see this love? It is not a love of empty flattery that gives trinkets of affection with no real intimacy. Our love is to be different than that seen in the world at large. What do we do to demonstrate love in such a way that the world will notice and give glory to God? We've often heard it said, "Love is a verb." A verb is an action word. Being there, really present, when people are in distress means you are **not** on your cell phone but truly listening and caring lovingly. Another demonstration of love is meeting material needs. The church members taking food, clothing, and even money to families in a time of crisis is an action visible to non-Christians. We can take care of someone's children while they are at the hospital with their spouse or another child. Mowing an elderly member's lawn, taking someone shopping or delivering groceries to someone confined to home due to age or illness, praying with a brother or sister are all visible acts of love. If you are unable to get out, you can pray over the phone with another believer to encourage them, write a note in a card and mail it, or even communicate as we do today (since the Covid-19 pandemic) by taking advantage of social media outlets or Zoom™, GoogleMeet™, Skype™, and Facetime™.

If you think about it for a few minutes, we are sure you can find a way to love your brother or sister in Christ! Ask the Lord to show you who needs an outward demonstration of God's love through you today.

Father, help us to be "Jesus with skin on" to a brother or sister in Christ that a lost and dying world might see our acts of love and be drawn to Jesus. Let us be known by our love for one another.

DOES THE LORD MAKE HIS HOME WITH YOU?

Whoever has My commandments and keeps them is the one who loves[G25] *Me. The one who loves*[G25] *Me will be loved*[G25] *by My Father, and I will love him and reveal Myself to him." . . .*

Jesus replied, "If anyone loves[G25] *Me, he will keep My word. My Father will love*[G25] *him, and We will come to him and make Our home with him. Whoever does not love*[G25] *Me does not keep My words. The word that you hear is not My own, but it is from the Father who sent Me.*

John 14:21, 23-24

To know Jesus is to believe He is the Son of God who is the only way to salvation (John 14:6). When we love Jesus, we get to know Him more deeply by reading His word which should lead us to obey what we have read in His word. Jesus said He and the Father would love those who believe and keep God's word and would take up residence—make their dwelling place—within him or her. They will abide in the believer, and the believer will abide in them. We are not sure the disciples understood this concept of the Lord dwelling with them even after He was no longer on earth in bodily form. However, this truth would become a pillar of their faith after the resurrection and ascension of Jesus as seen in the book of Acts. In Acts chapter two, the Holy Spirit came to dwell in the believers gathered in an upper room to pray. Since that time, the Holy Spirit has entered each new believer in Jesus. The Lord being present in our lives is what carries us through each day. The converse is also true: when you reject Jesus, you are rejecting God the Father. God sent Jesus as His representative to enlighten humanity about the Father's attributes by seeing Him in living color, flesh-and-blood. Therefore, they could relate to and understand Him as a man. Jesus said many times that He spoke only that which the Father told Him. Therefore, to discard Jesus's words is to discard God's words. To disobey Jesus is to disobey Father God.

Are you keenly aware of the Holy Spirit's presence in your life? If not, check two things:

1. Have you trusted Jesus alone for salvation, believing Him to be the Son of God who died on the cross for your sins and was raised from the dead to reign with the Father? If not, you must start at this point. The pastor of a Bible believing church would be happy to help you solidify your relationship with the Lord. Or you can contact us through our website www.preciousjewelsministries.com

2. Are you studying God's word, the Bible, and obeying what the Lord shows you as you read? "Draw near to God, and He will draw near to you. Cleanse your hands, you sinners, and purify

your hearts, you double-minded" (James 4:8). We draw near when we read and obey His word.

Father, help us to be in Your word daily and obey whatever You show us there. Forgive us when we fall short, cleanse us, and set us back on the path You have chosen for us.

REMAIN IN THE
REDEEMER'S LOVE

*As the Father has loved[G25] Me, so have I loved[G25] you.
Remain in My love.[G26] If you keep My commandments,
you will remain in My love,[G26] just as I have kept My
Father's commandments and remain in His love.[G26]*

John 15:9-10

Jesus has loved us as He is loved by the Father. God's love is perfect, unconditional, and everlasting. Jesus's love for us was manifested when he died on the cross to pay the debt we owed because of our sin. We did not earn or deserve His sacrifice: He chose to take our place because of love and in obedience to God the Father. We are to remain, reside, and be rooted in His love. What does that look like? Jesus states that "If you keep My commandments, you will remain in My love." Jesus kept His Father's commandments perfectly and completely. He was obedient even to death on the cross as we are told in Philippians chapter two. When we obey what is taught in the Bible, we become ever closer to Jesus and even more aware of His abiding love for us. Our salvation is completely by grace through faith that God chose to give us. We cannot lose what Christ died for! However, daily walking in the Spirit, choosing to obey God's word, intensifies our understanding of the love we have *from* God and *for* God. Remaining in His love is accomplished through obedience to God's will.

> *Psalm 139:23-24 Search me, O God, and know my heart; test me and know my concerns. See if there is any offensive way in me; lead me in the way everlasting.*

Do we dare to pray this prayer of David each day and then change our lives to line up with whatever God shows us? Do we dare to be obedient to the Lord's will and ways even when that path seems harder than the one we are currently on? We are quick to ask God to supply things we need, but are we seeking Him above all? "But seek first the kingdom of God and His righteousness, and all these things will be added unto you" (Matt. 6:33). Seek the Lord in earnest prayer this week. Then move forward in obedience to what the Holy Spirit shows you through God's word, the Bible.

Father, by the power of Your Holy Spirit living inside us, help us to live in obedience to Your commands as a demonstration of our love for You and our desire to remain in You, our Redeemer, the Lord Jesus Christ.

LOVE IS LAYING DOWN
OUR LIVES

This is My commandment, that you love^G25 one another as I have loved^G25 you. Greater love^G26 has no one than this, that he lay down his life for his friends. . . This is My command to you: Love^G25 one another.

John 15:12-13, 17

J esus's disciples—those who trust in Him and are being conformed to His image—are to live out His love to others, loving not only in word but in action. The admonition set forth by Jesus—the command for daily living for Christ-followers—is that they demonstrate an active love toward one another in imitation of the love Jesus has lavished upon them. As children imitate their parents, we are to imitate the Lord. How did Jesus love and to what extent? Jesus loved sacrificially, unconditionally, and purely. He loved with everything—His heart, mind, and soul. He went so far as to die for those He loved. And now, He continues to make intercession for us at the throne of God. Jesus expresses His love for us forever!!!

Rom. 8:34 Who is there to condemn us? For Christ Jesus, who died, and more than that was raised to life, is at the

> *right hand of God—and He is interced-*
> *ing for us.*

An important reflection on John 15:13 is that Jesus is addressing His friends, the community of faith. The word for friends in this verse could be interpreted "beloved ones." This indicates an intimate friendship, a family relationship, or as we like to call it "framily" which means friends who have become family through Jesus. As stated in Proverbs 18:24 (NIV) "...there is a friend who sticks closer than a brother." Even before Jesus willingly laid down His life on the cross, He set aside the splendor of Heaven to be born to a humble couple and live life as a man that we might understand the Father's love through His example. The price of Jesus's love culminated in the crucifixion—His sacrificial death as a substitute for those He loved.

We may not literally lay down our lives for our "framily"—our brothers and sisters in Christ. However, we need to be willing to love sacrificially by preferring others before ourselves. This week, watch for an opportunity to do something for or with a loved one even though it might not be your own "cup of tea." Consider giving up some "me time," in favor of "us time." Think of ways to love sacrificially.

Father, please remove selfishness from us and help us to put others' needs before our own. We realize we are to love ourselves, but this should never be at the ex-

pense of others. Let Your love flow through us to our friends and family, especially those who are brothers and sisters in Christ.

TWO TYPES OF LOVE

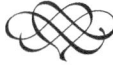

G25 – *agapáō* – To esteem, love, indicating a direction of the will and finding one's joy in something or someone . . . Agapáō and never philéō is used of love toward our enemies. The range of philéō is wider than of agapáō which stands higher than philéō because of its moral import, i.e., love that expresses compassion. We are thus commanded to love (agapáō) our enemies, to do what is necessary to turn them to Christ, but never to befriend them (philéō) by adopting their interests and becoming friends on their level. [5]

G5368 – *philéō* – Loved, dear, friend. To love. Generally . . . to have affection for someone. . . Believers are never told to love their enemies with the word philéō because that would mean to have the same interests as they have. [6]

We can choose to love our enemies,
but only with *agapáō*, please.
We are cordial to them and do kind deeds,
praying that surrender to Jesus, it leads.
We cannot become the best of buddies
because joining in sin our witness muddies.
We cannot share interests that do not glorify
our Lord Jesus who for us chose to die.

We philéō our brothers and sisters in Christ
who share our goal to lead godly lives.
We can be best friends with those who love Jesus,
Enjoying the bond of His grace that frees us.
However, we also *agapáō* these friends
knowing our enjoyment of them never ends.
Our love of believers even when disagreeing
is the kind of love the world needs to be seeing.

DO YOU LOVE ME, PETER?

When they had finished eating, Jesus asked Simon Pe-
ter, "Simon son of John, do you love^{G25} Me more than
these?" "Yes, Lord," he answered, "You know I love^{G5368}
You." Jesus replied, "Feed My lambs."

John 21:15

Why did Jesus single out Peter from the other Apostles? Peter was the one in need of restoration. Jesus had already forgiven Peter, but Peter had not forgiven himself and needed reassurance that Jesus had
forgiven him. Peter was also the Lord's choice to lead
the early church, to help them keep their focus on the
Gospel—the Good News—and begin the task of spread-
ing it all over the world. Jesus asked Peter if he loved
Him more than the others. He used the term for moral, willing, choice to love regardless of feelings—agapáō.
How did Peter answer Him? Peter answered that he felt
brotherly love and affection—phileō—for the Lord. Jesus already knew Peter's heart but was helping Peter
to examine himself. This kind of love was all Peter or
anyone else was able to have without the indwelling of
the Holy Spirit which was to come a while later during
the feast of Pentecost. What did Jesus mean when He
told Peter to feed His lambs? Jesus let Peter know that
he had the authority to carry the Gospel message as a
witness, and He was counting on him to do so by the

power of the Holy Spirit working in and through him to do His will, to feed His sheep—the followers of Jesus. What would feeding Jesus' lambs consist of? Peter was to make disciples, teaching (feeding) them everything Jesus had commanded all the Apostles:

> *Matt. 28:18-20 Then Jesus came to them and said, "All authority in heaven and on earth has been given to Me. Therefore go and make disciples of all nations, baptizing them in the name of the Father, and of the Son, and of the Holy Spirit, and teaching them to obey all that I have commanded you. And surely I am with you always, even to the end of the age."*

We feed Christ's lambs when we teach them God's word and teach them to internalize scripture to be enabled to live it out (obey it) as a testimony to others. We learned in John 13:34-35 that believers are to be known by their love—agapáō. Part of loving this way is to help other believers grow in their relationship to the Source of love, Jesus. We are to make disciples—believers being made into the likeness of Christ. We can only willfully choose to love people—even when we do not have a brotherly or sisterly affection for them—when the Holy Spirit is living in us. Love check: Are you able to choose love when someone is difficult to love—to love unconditionally? Or are you only able to show a love based on mutual affection? Ask the Lord to infuse you with His kind of love—*agapáō*.

Father, help us to love as You love—willingly, sacrificially, and unconditionally. May Your Holy Spirit within us lead us to love others as You have loved us.

DO YOU LOVE ME, PETER? 2.0

Jesus asked a second time, "Simon son of John, do you love^G25 Me?" "Yes, Lord," he answered, "You know I love^G5368 You." Jesus told him, "Shepherd My sheep."

John 21:16

Jesus knew that Peter would eventually be able to truly say he had the self-sacrificing, deliberate choice type of love (*agapáō*) for Jesus. He posed the same question again. Peter again answered honestly that he felt brotherly love (*phileō*) for Jesus. This time Jesus commanded Peter to "tend" or "shepherd" his sheep. Is there a difference between feeding and tending the sheep? Anyone can carry dinner to the sheep. Tending has more of a connotation of nurturing and preserving. Tending the sheep involves inspecting for injuries, watching out for infestations, protecting from dangerous predators, caring for every aspect of the lamb. The shepherd puts his own life in harm's way on behalf of the sheep. David fought off lions and bears who preyed on his father's sheep. The shepherd is both nurse and nurturer for the flock. Therefore, Jesus was telling Peter to shepherd the believers, the early church. He did so in his teaching at Pentecost, his leadership of the early church being sure believers dined on the word of God, and later in his letters warning of false teachers (predators) and admonishing the church to stay true to the things Jesus taught even amid persecution.

Jesus knew that to truly shepherd His flock—the body of believers—Peter would need to love both Jesus and His sheep. This would necessitate Godly love—agapáō—which Peter did not yet have. Peter still answered that he had brotherly affection for Jesus—phileō. Peter knew there was no way he could embrace the God-type of love even for the God-man, Jesus, in his humanity. However, Jesus, being omniscient, knew that He would soon be sending the Holy Spirit to enter Peter enabling him to follow the command to love—*agapáō*—and tend His sheep.

Do you love—*apapáō*—the Lord at all times? Or is the measure of your love contingent upon His answering your prayers in the way you think He should? The kind of love Jesus was asking Peter to have for Him and for His sheep was not dependent on circumstances. If we cannot love Jesus unconditionally, how can we love messy human beings in this way? Only the Holy Spirit can teach us to love in this way. Ask Him to increase and elevate your love capacity!

Father, by Your Holy Spirit increase Your love in us. Help us, daily, to choose to love others. Remind us to express our love for You through obedience, worship, prayer, and Bible study.

SIMON PETER, IS THIS YOUR FINAL ANSWER?

Jesus asked a third time, "Simon son of John, do you love[G5368] Me?" Peter was deeply hurt that Jesus had asked him a third time, "Do you love[G5368] Me?" "Lord, You know all things," he replied. "You know I love[G5368] You." Jesus said to him, "Feed My sheep.

John 21:17

W hy did Jesus ask Peter if he loved Him three times? Jesus knew that Peter was still bearing guilt and beating himself up every day because he had denied knowing the Lord three times to complete strangers on the night Jesus was betrayed and arrested. At the time Jesus needed his friends the most, Peter denied ever knowing Him. Jesus was absolving Peter of that guilt by giving him the opportunity to affirm his love for Him the same number of times he denied him. Is it significant that Jesus changed from agapáō to philéō when He asked the third time whether Peter loved Him? Perhaps Jesus was acknowledging that Peter was not yet fully capable of God-like love and was being respectful of Peter's honest response that he had brotherly affection. Jesus knew that after the Holy Spirit filled Peter at Pentecost, he would be infused with agapáō. Why was Peter grieved that Jesus asked him if he loved (philéō) Him the third time? Maybe Peter was grieved and embarrassed because he knew that he could not love Jesus with *agapáō* love yet, and he wanted to. Peter acknowledged that Jesus knew everything and already knew he loved him as a brother. Jesus again instructed Peter to feed the sheep. Is there a significance to the fact that He did this three times? Peter had denied Jesus three times, humiliating himself because he had been one of the three men closest to the Lord and had even bragged that he would follow Jesus to the death. Therefore, Jesus entrusted His followers to Peter three times to show him that he was completely restored to his position of leadership within the band of Apostles.

If you are a born-again believer, you are inhabited by the Holy Spirit who entered your life as soon as you surrendered to God's call to be His child. From that moment we begin growing. The more we know Jesus through the study of His word, spending time in prayer, and meditating on what He has shown us, the more His love will flow through us. We are empowered to love because Jesus has first loved us (more on that when we look at 1 John 4:19). However, even though we have the power to love, we often do not "plug in" to the power source of love. Earnestly pray to love more completely, love more like Jesus, and tune in to the Holy Spirit's prompting. He will enable you to do everything He has called you to do, even to agapáō the Lord and those in His forever family. Pray that the river of His love will flow like rapids in and through your life and spill over onto all who come in contact with you.

Father, the Lord Jesus told His disciples that men would know they belonged to Him because of their visible love for each other. We pray a tidal wave of agapáō will engulf us, and others would see Jesus in us.

OVERFLOWING OUTPOURING OF GOD'S LOVE

And hope does not disappoint us, because God has poured out His love[G26] *into our hearts through the Holy Spirit, whom He has given us.*

Rom. 5:5

5:5 love of God . . . poured out. God's love for us (cf. v. 8) has been lavishly poured out to the point of overflowing within our hearts. [7]

When God pours out His love, it is not a mere trickle or even a barrel full. God's love for us is a powerful waterfall, continually flowing through believers in the person of His Holy Spirit. We are to share that overflowing love with others and never try to dam up the flow, i.e. quench the Spirit (1 Thessalonians 5:19). We are not designed to hold the love just for ourselves but to allow it to flow through us to others. The Holy Spirit is described by Jesus in John 7:38 (NLT), "Anyone who believes in me may come and drink! For the Scriptures declare, 'Rivers of living water will flow from his heart.'" The love of God that we share with others is sincere and cannot be faked. "Don't just pretend to love others. Really love them" (Rom. 12:9a). When the authentic, unconditional love of God invades our hearts, we must share it with other people (unbelievers as well as brothers and sisters in Christ) or explode!

If your love for others seems to be down to a trickle, you need to return to the Source of that love. It is an indication that your relationship to the Lord Jesus may not be on track, and the flow of His love is obstructed. Perhaps there is unconfessed sin blocking the channel of blessing like silt in a river. 1 John 1:9 is the remedy for the blockage: "If we confess our sins, He is faithful and just to forgive us our sins and to cleanse us from all unrighteousness." Jesus said people would know we belong to Him when they see our love for one another (John 13:35). Take stock of how well you are demonstrating God's love to others, both believers and those who need to come to a saving knowledge of Christ. How can you demonstrate His love today?

Father, help us to never be guilty of quenching the Holy Spirit instead of allowing Him to flow freely through us. May the evidence of His presence—the Fruit of the Spirit, beginning with love—be a consistent testimony of Your grace in our lives.

VICTORIOUS SACRIFICIAL LOVE

For at just the right time, while we were still power-less, Christ died for the ungodly. Very rarely will any-one die for a righteous man, though for a good man someone might possibly dare to die. But God proves His love[G26] for us in this: While we were still sinners, Christ died for us.

Rom. 5:6-8

We were powerless to save ourselves,
Incapable, constantly missing the mark.
We needed a vessel to save us from destruction
Just as sure as Noah needed the ark.
Although we were completely unworthy,
God sent His Son Jesus to die
Because the only way to purify us
Was through a sinless sacrifice.
So while we were still ungodly,
Incapable of overcoming sin,
God proved His unconditional love
By sending Jesus to walk among men.
Jesus obeyed the Father completely
And lived a sinless life.

He was the perfect, spotless Lamb
Required for the sacrifice.
Christ willingly gave His life for us.
While we were sinners, died in our place.
Because of the Father's infinite love,
We will someday see Christ face to face.
Our Savior rose from the dead as He said,
For death could not conquer our Champion.
Just as He rose, we will someday arise,
Victorious, because of His passion.
And then we will join Him
In the place He's preparing
And forever and ever
His joy we'll be sharing.

WHAT IS GOOD?

*And we know that God works all things together
for the good^G18 of those who love^G25 Him, who are
called according to His purpose.For those God fore-
knew, He also predestined to be conformed to the
image of His Son, so that He would be the firstborn
among many brothers.*

Rom. 8:28-29

> G18 *agathós* - (C) Of abstract things: tó
> agathón, something useful and profit-
> able, beneficial (Rom. 8:28; 12:21; 13:4;
> Gal. 6:10; Eph. 4:28; 6:8; 1 Thess. 5:15;
> Phile. 1:6, 14). [8]

First, we must point out that this promise is only ap-
plicable to those who love God and have answered
His call to trust Jesus as their Savior. Most believers are
familiar with Rom. 8:28, but many do not read on to
the next verse. God works all the circumstances of our
lives together for our good. Exactly what is the "good"?
We tend to envision health, wealth, and an easy road
as good. According to the definition above, good in this
context is something useful, profitable, and beneficial.
If we read on to verse 29, we see that the "good" that
God wants for us is to be "conformed to the image of His
Son." He works even the situations we perceive as "bad"

to develop Christ-like character in us. There is no higher good than to be more like Jesus! The Holy Spirit is active in the lives of those who love God to produce His fruit in them: "But the fruit of the Spirit is love, joy, peace, patience, kindness, goodness, faithfulness, gentleness, and self-control" (Galatians 5:22-23a). Having the Holy Spirit flow through us developing these character traits to improve our relationships and our witness to the world is definitely for our benefit. God designed us to be His ambassadors to the world, performing good works in His name. "For we are God's workmanship, created in Christ Jesus to do good works, which God prepared in advance as our way of life" (Ephesians 2:10).

When examining yourself, do you see God working the good of being more like His Son into you? If not, ask the Father to infuse you with the Holy Spirit's power to produce the Fruit of the Spirit. Developing these Christ-like qualities will definitely be beneficial not only for the Kingdom of God, but for you personally.

Father, help us to take an inventory of our own attitudes and actions. Where our lives do not match the truth of Your word, enable us to change. Help us to be made more and more like Jesus for this is Your divine benefit, our ultimate destiny.

UNFAILING, EVERLASTING LOVE

Who shall separate us from the love^{G26} of Christ?
Shall trouble or distress or persecution or famine or
nakedness or danger or sword? As it is written:"For
Your sake we face death all day long; we are con-
sidered as sheep to be slaughtered." No, in all these
things we are more than conquerors through Him who
loved^{G25} us. For I am convinced that neither death nor
life, neither angels nor principalities, neither the pres-
ent nor the future, nor any powers, neither height nor
depth, nor anything else in all creation, will be able
to separate us from the love^{G26} of God that is in Christ
Jesus our Lord.

Roman 8:35-39

We are only able to love as God commands us to because He first loved us (1 John 4:19). We will never lose the power to love others because we can never be
separated from God's love. His love is continually made
known to us by His Holy Spirit who inhabits us. The list
of beings, things, and abstract concepts that CANNOT
separate us from the love of God is comprehensive: trouble, distress, persecution, famine, nakedness, danger, or
sword. Then Paul continues to describe what is unable
to put a gap between us and God's love with a series of
merisms—using two contrasting parts to represent the

whole including everything in between the two—life/ death, angels/principalities, present/future, height/ depth. To make sure we understand that NOTHING can separate us from God's love, Paul adds, "nor any powers" and "nor anything else in all creation." Whew! We are completely secure and enveloped in God's incomparable, unconditional, unmerited love. Nothing we can imagine can cause God to stop loving us, not even ourselves! Once we have trusted Jesus and surrendered our lives to Him, we are held tightly by God's grace.

> *John 10:28-29 I give them eternal life, and they will never perish. No one can snatch them out of My hand. My Father who has given them to Me is greater than all. No one can snatch them out of My Father's hand.*

God loves you and will never stop loving you. Therefore, the Holy Spirit will continue to give you the ability to love others. Are you resting peacefully in God's unfailing, everlasting love? Love is first in the list of the Fruit of the Spirit because all the other Christlike traits stem from the love God has placed in our hearts. Intentionally plan to share that love with others this week. Say or write an encouraging word to someone. Perform a chore for someone who is unable to do it themselves. Listen to a friend who is struggling. Hug your family and remind them God loves them no matter what.

Father, we are completely secure in Your love. Since You are the Source of love, we can love others. Help us to demonstrate Your love to others consistently.

AUTHENTIC LOVE

Love^{G26} must be sincere^{G505}.

Rom. 12:9a

The King James Version translates this verse, "Let love be without dissimulation." Susie asked what is "dissimulation?" We looked it up in our favorite English dictionary and looked up the Hebrew word in *Strong's*:

> DISSIMULATION, noun [Latin, to make like; like.] The act of dissembling; a hiding under a false appearance; a feigning; false pretension; hypocrisy. dissimulation may be simply concealment of the opinions, sentiments or purpose; but it includes also the assuming of a false or counterfeit appearance which conceals the real opinions or purpose. [9]

> G505 -*anypókritos* - undissembled, i.e. sincere:—without dissimulation (hypocrisy), unfeigned. [10]

Love must be authentic. It must not have the stench of hypocrisy about it. Loving as the Lord loves us is not something you can "fake it 'til you make it." Therefore, if we are having a difficult time loving our brothers and sisters in Christ or showing God's love to an unbeliever for the purpose of pointing them to Jesus, we must stop and pray. As we have stated many times before, we cannot love the way God commands us to love in our own strength. We cannot muster up a loving feeling toward someone who completely drives us crazy. Agápē (willful love) is a choice we make, but we can only make that choice by the power of the Holy Spirit living within us. Sometimes, the ability to love a person is a daily or even moment by moment request before the Lord and a surrender to His will.

When the first Christian martyr was being stoned to death, he cried out, "Lord, do not hold this sin against them" (Acts 7:60b). The only way he could love those men enough to pray for God to forgive them was because he was "was full of grace and power" (Acts 6:8b). In other words, the Holy Spirit empowered Stephen to love.

Think right now about a person or persons you find it difficult to truly love or even be nice to at times. Ask the Lord to fill you with a sincere love for him or her and the strength to show kindness to them. Pray for that person desiring that they be brought into closer relationship with Jesus. We believe God will then enable you to demonstrate His love.

Father, help us to love others as You command. Help us to resist exercising a "faky" love thinking we are fooling someone. We cannot fool You. Help our love to be sincere, without hypocrisy.

BROTHERLY/SISTERLY LOVE

Be devoted[G5387] *to one another in brotherly love*[G5360].
Outdo yourselves in honoring one another.

Rom. 12:10

G5387 - *philóstorgos*; from G5384 and στοργ *storgé* (cherishing one's kindred, especially parents or children); fond of natural relatives, i.e. fraternal towards fellow Christians:—kindly affectioned. [11]

G5360 – *philadelphía*; from G5361; fraternal affection:—brotherly love (kindness), love of the brethren. [12]

We can see that the Greek words for "devotion" and "brotherly love" in this verse derive from G5368 philéō. Christians are a family, the family of God. Being a part of the family of God or as we like to say, "familyship," involves brotherly/sisterly love. As a familyship, we have the same Father (God), the same goal (furthering His kingdom by fulfilling His purposes), the same responsibility (to love Him with all our heart, soul, and mind and to love our neighbors). We have a stronger bond than just "teammates." We are born into an earthly family, and even though we eventually move out of home and begin a home of our own, we are still connected to our parents and siblings. When we are born into the family of God, we are all connected by our One Love;

and no matter where we roam on this earth, we never move completely away from the family of God because we can find other believers wherever we travel. Our parents insisted we "get along" with our siblings and work together as a family. The Lord expects us to do more than just keep a semblance of peace with our brothers and sisters in Christ. He instructs us to "outdo" each other in showing kindness to our Christian siblings. The Apostle Paul under the divine guidance of the Holy Spirt taught often about unity in the body (family) of Christ. Here, he is teaching us to be demonstrative in our love for one another. After all, as we have seen in earlier devotions, that is how non-believers will recognize us as Christians (John 13:35).

In many ways, our brothers and sisters in Christ can become even closer than our biological family members, especially if we came from a dysfunctional home. This week, brainstorm ways to "outdo" each other in showing love within the family of God. Kind words and deeds will strengthen our bonds with other believers.

Father, help us to work at outdoing each other in showing brotherly/sisterly love to our Christian family. Infuse us with a desire to be the best siblings possible. May we be a testimony of love and unity in a world filled with hate and discord.

BROTHERLY LOVE

Susan and her brother-in-Christ, Jon, on her 50ᵗʰ birthday.

Be devoted[G5387] to one another in brotherly love[G5360].
Outdo yourselves in honoring one another.

Rom. 12:10

Now about brotherly love[G5360], you do not need any-
one to write to you, because you yourselves have been
taught by God to love[G25] one another.

I Thessalonians 4:9

Characterized by brotherly love:

That's how we should be known.

Christians should be people

Who take care of their own.

Our kindness toward each other,

Our help in time of need,

Can touch the hearts of many lost

And plant a tiny seed.

For what our neighbors see in us

And in our Christian friends,

Should make them want to know the Lord

On whom we all depend.

THE NEVER-ENDING DEBT!!!

*Be indebted to no one, except to one another in love[G25].
For he who loves[G25] his neighbor has fulfilled the law.
The commandments "Do not commit adultery," "Do
not murder," "Do not steal," "Do not covet," and any
other commandments, are summed up in this one
decree: "Love[G25] your neighbor as yourself." Love[G26]
does no wrong to its neighbor. Therefore love[G26] is the
fulfillment of the law.*

Rom. 13:8-10

Susan and I recently paid off all our credit card debt.
Considering it was over $15,000.00 when we first
became roommates nearly eight years ago, that is a ma-
jor Praise the Lord! Debt is like a weight holding one
down and keeping one from so many things. This verse
teaches that we should pay in a timely manner when we
incur a debt. However, there is one debt that is never
"paid in full." That is our obligation to love others. This
love is not limited to our brothers and sisters in Christ
but is extended to our "neighbors." As we have seen before, our neighbor is anyone who enters our sphere of
influence ranging from our literal neighbor next door to
the sack boy at the grocery store to the homeless person
we pass by every day on our way to work. Love here is
agapáō or agápē meaning a willful choice of compassion
because of our moral obligation to the Lord. We will

never completely pay this debt because, as this passage points out, loving our neighbor fulfills all the commandments concerning our relationships with others because love does no harm. John 15:13 tells us that there is no greater love than to lay down one's life for one's friends. Jesus loved us so much that He willingly suffered and died on the cross in His incarnate, fully human yet fully God state. He felt and endured every blow of the scourge, each nail pounded into His flesh, and the slow suffocation of being nailed to the cross because He loved us. We must realize that we could never completely repay that debt! Praise the Lord that in His grace He does not expect us to repay it fully. However, He does command us to continually pay on that debt by sharing His love with others. When we allow His Holy Spirit to flow through us to share love with others, we draw closer to Him and hear His direction for us more clearly.

If the debt of love came with a booklet of payment slips, it would be endless. Challenge yourself to consciously make daily payments on the debt of love even knowing it can never fully be repaid. However, the reward for making these payments is great, and someday you will hear, "Well done, good and faithful servant . . . Enter into the joy of your master!" (Matt. 25:21)

Father, we know we will never get to the end of the love payment book. Please empower us to pay on the debt of love each day in our homes with our families, with neighbors, and by loving those You place in our paths as divine appointments to demonstrate Your love in order to lead the lost to You. Thank You for the grace that frees us from sin and allows us to dwell in Your everlasting love.

NOTHING WITHOUT LOVE

If I speak in the tongues of men and of angels, but have not love[G26], I am only a ringing gong or a clanging cymbal. If I have the gift of prophecy and can fathom all mysteries and all knowledge, and if I have absolute faith so as to move mountains, but have not love[G26], I am nothing. If I give all I possess to the poor and exult in the surrender of my body, but have not love[G26], I gain nothing.

1 Corinthians 13:1-3

No gift, talent, or character quality has real substance without love. If I am speaking eloquently or even in tongues but am devoid of love, I'm just obnoxiously noisy. If I can speak truth with all understanding and even if I have faith strong enough to move mountains, but I do not have love, I am nothing—worthless. If I am generous to the point of giving everything I have and am even martyred for my faith, and do not have love, there is nothing to gain from all my sacrifice. Love must be the foundational motivation behind exercising any of my God-given gifts. The bottom line is that our spiritual gifts remain ineffective if the use of them is not motivated by love for God first and then for others. We are to surrender ourselves to God as instruments of His love. Love must be the conduit through which our God-given gifts flow.

As you exercise your gifts, do a heart-check to make sure you are doing so out of love. If your gift is teaching, are you teaching because you love your students? If you are helping someone, is it out of duty or sense of obligation, or is it from a heart of love for God and others? If you are preaching the word of God, is it because it is your job or because God has given you a love and concern for others? If you are being merciful, is it motivated by pity or love? Pray with us that God infuses you with His love and His power to share that love in all you do.

> *Philippians 4:13 AMP I can do all things [which He has called me to do] through Him who strengthens and empowers me [to fulfill His purpose—I am self-sufficient in Christ's sufficiency; I am ready for anything and equal to anything through Him who infuses me with inner strength and confident peace.]*

Father, You infuse us with Your strength to accomplish all You have called us to do. We pray to be filled with Your love for others and to let that love motivate us to use the many gifts and resources You have graciously given us to bless others and to bring glory to Your name.

LOVE IS . . .

Love^{G26} is patient ^{G3114}, love is kind^{G5541} . . .
1 Corinthians 13:4a

Before we go further into the "love chapter," I (Susan) want to share with you what I was impressed to do with these verses. I began by substituting "Jesus" for "love", as in Jesus is patient, etc. Then, since we are supposed to be imitators of Jesus (Ephesians 5:1), I substituted my own name in each statement: "Susan is patient." As you do this, examine yourself to see how well you are living up to the Lord's definition of love.

> G3114 - *makrothyméō* – To suffer long, be long-suffering, as opposed to hasty anger or punishment (1 Cor.13:4; 1 Thess. 5:14, 2 Peter 3:9) . . . *Makrothuméō* involves exercising understanding and patience toward persons while *hupoménō (G5278)* involves putting up with things or circumstances. [13]

Love exercises understanding and patience toward people. It is a choice to not let anger flare up but instead to be "quick to listen, slow to speak, and slow to anger" (James 1:19). Do I eagerly strain toward understanding rather than giving place to a knee-jerk reaction that causes divisiveness rather than unity? Jesus has certainly exercised patience with me! Now, by the power of the Holy Spirit, I can choose to love others by being patient with them.

> G5541 -*chrēsteúomai* – useful. To be kind, obliging, willing to help or assist (1 Co. 13:4) [14]

Love is "willing to help or assist." It is useful. Kindness is not just a feeling toward someone but is springing into action on their behalf. "God's kindness leads you to repentance" (Rom. 2:4b). We cannot enter into a relationship with the Lord unless in His kindness, he draws us to Himself to be reconciled to Him. One way God demonstrates kindness toward us is by providing for our daily needs—food, shelter, etc. Am I being the hands and feet of Jesus by assisting others in their time of need? We are thinking right now of a precious friend of ours who went out of his way to pick up the groceries we had ordered online for ourselves and for my mom and then deliver them to each of our homes because we were not feeling well. He showed kindness to us by being useful, helpful, and available.

Father, as we study the definitions of love in I Corinthians 13, help us to examine ourselves to see where our love falls short. Help us courageously ask You to infuse us with Your love and enable us to act on what we learn.

LOVE DOES NOT AND IS NOT . . .

It does not envy[G2206], it does not boast[G4068], it is not proud[G5448].

1 Corinthians 13:4b

G2206 *zēlóō* – to envy, be moved with envy (Acts 7:9; 1 Cor.13:4; James 4:2) [15]

envy (verb) - desire to have a quality, possession, or other desirable attribute belonging to (someone else). [16]

Love prefers the other person rather than craving what he or she has. Love does not need to have everything the other person has to feel fulfilled. On the contrary, love desires the highest and best for the person that is loved. We must ask ourselves, "Do we put others above ourselves? Do we crave something or some trait of another person to the point of disliking him or her because they possess something we do not?" Envy can lead to hate, the opposite of love and godliness because "God is love" (1 John 4:8). Do we recognize envy as sin and ask the Lord to cleanse us?

G4068 *perpereúomai* – braggart, to brag or boast [17]

Love (remember to substitute your own name) does not brag or boast. Are we always expounding on our own accomplishments, or do we enjoy celebrating the accomplishments of others? Paul cautions us elsewhere, "Do not think of yourself more highly than you ought," (Rom. 12:3b). God has given each of us gifts *not* that we should think ourselves better than others but to be used for the betterment of others. We are to humbly use the gifts we have been given to serve the Lord by serving others.

G5448 *phusióō* – to breath, blow, inflate. To inflate, blow or puff up. In the NT spoken only figuratively of pride or self-conceit. [18]

If we are puffed up with pride and completely self-centered, how can we possibly show love to our neighbor? The Christ-like love spoken of here—agapáō—is a self-sacrificing love. It is a love that denies oneself to follow Christ and to bless others. Love is not proud. Now put your name in the place of "Love," as in, Susan is not proud. Is the statement true of you?

Father, help us not to be envious, boastful, or proud. Help us instead to be contented and humble. Help us to remember what Paul taught Timothy, ". . . godliness with contentment is great gain," (1 Timothy 6:6) and live accordingly.

LOVE IS NOT . . .

It is not rude[G809], it is not self-seeking[G2212], it is not easily angered[G3947], it keeps no account[G3049] of wrongs.

1 Corinthians 13:5

G809 *aschēmonéō* – uncomely, indecent [19]

Love is not rude. "Uncomely" reminds me (Susie) of something my grandma would say, "That behavior is not becoming of a young lady." Love never behaves in a way that is "unbecoming." My (Susan's) Grannie would say it this way: "Pretty is as pretty does."

G2212 *zētéō* – to seek, in the sense of endeavor, to try, e.g. followed by the acc. Of thing, to try to gain, to strive after, with the idea of earnestness and anxiety (1 Cor.10:24) [20]

Love is not in the relationship merely for what can be gained from it. Love exemplifies being a "giver" rather than a "taker." Love is not "out to get something." It is not seeking self-gratification. Love demonstrates gratitude.

G3947 *paroxýnō* - . . . In the NT, it means to provoke or rouse to anger or indignation . . . [21]

Love (are you remembering to insert your own name?) does not fly off the handle at the least provocation. Love is thoughtfully responsive rather than instantly reactive.

G3049 *logízomai* - Actually, the verb *logízomai* means to put together with one's mind, to count, to occupy oneself with reckonings or calculations. [22]

Love does not set itself up as the good behavior/bad behavior accountant. It does not keep a list of every time a person has offended or wronged them to be thrown up to the person any time there is an argument. Susie's former pastor would admonish the bride and groom in the wedding ceremony to always "fight fair." He would explain that only the issue at hand should be discussed rather than dredging up an entire list of previous offenses. Wow! Can I truly put my name there? Susie keeps no account of wrongs. Honestly, this can be a stumbling block for me because I have a long memory.

Father, taking an honest look at what it means to truly love—agápē—others and examining ourselves in light of those definitions is convicting. Enable us by the power of Your Holy Spirit within us to be more conformed to the image of Christ in the area of loving others. Thank You for the gracious love You have extended to us!

LOVE (AGÁPĒ) DEFINED

*Love[G26] is patient, love[G26] is kind. It does not envy,
it does not boast, it is not proud. It is not rude, it is
not self-seeking, it is not easily angered, it keeps no
account of wrongs. Love[G26] takes no pleasure in evil,
but rejoices in the truth. It bears all things, believes
all things, hopes all things, endures all things. Love[G26]
never fails.*

1 Corinthians 13:4-8a

Paul wrote to the church at Corinth,
a letter in which love is defined.
After stating without love we are nothing,
he began with love is patient and kind.
Love does not envy. It does not boast.
Love is not proud nor rude.
Love is not self-seeking or easily angered.
Love does not list wrongs in a queue.
Love takes no pleasure in evil,
but it always rejoices in truth.
How am I doing living this love
that I have been taught from my youth?
Love bears all things, the trials of life.
Love believes all things, strong in trust.

Love hopes all things, not giving up.
Love patiently endures what it must.
Love never fails. True love never bails.
The love exemplified by Christ
measured up to all these definitions
consistently in His earthly life.
If I put the name of Jesus
in place of the word "love,"
I will see that He is the example
of everything this love does.
Another way to look at this list
is to substitute my own name.
Can I insert my name instead of "love?"
Can I live up to that claim?
I need to seek the Holy Spirit's power
to emulate the love of Christ,
For only as the Spirit flows through me
can love permeate my life.

LOVE DOES NOT REJOICE . . . BUT REJOICES . . .

Love^{G26} takes no pleasure^{G5463} in evil^{G93} but rejoices^{G4796} in the truth^{G225}.

1 Corinthians 13:6

. . . it does not rejoice at wrongdoing, but rejoices with the truth.

1 Corinthians 13:6 (ESV)

G5463 *chaírō* – with a preposition expressing the cause or occasion of joy. [23]

G93 *adikía* – injustice . . . 1 Cor. 13:6 could be taken as those material things that could be acquired through the employment of falsehood in defrauding others instead of telling the truth. [24]

G4796 *synchaírō* – to rejoice together, to share in another's joy . . . to congratulate [25]

G225 *alḗtheia* – conduct conformed to the truth, integrity, probity, virtue, a life conformed to the precepts of the gospel . . . in Rom. 2:8 and 1 Cor. 13:6, *alḗtheia* stands in opposition to *adikía*, unrighteousness, wrong. [26]

The pattern throughout much of 1 Corinthians 13 is to state a negative followed by the positive. Here, love does *not* take joy in any kind of evil or injustice even if that evil is being perpetrated upon an enemy. Love never desires that someone else be hurt or suffer. Positively, love rejoices with those who are moving closer toward life and godliness, the sinner who is turning to Christ for salvation and sanctification. Love shares in the joy of another who is experiencing blessings. Love has no relationship with injustice. Love's behavior reflects integrity and virtue and is being "conformed to the image of His son" (Rom. 8:29).

If we are honest with ourselves, are there times when we are glad someone else got his or her "comeuppance," their "just deserts?" Do we desire punishment for evildoers more than grace and mercy? Are we like Jonah who did not want to take God's warning to the Ninevites because of their evil deeds? If we are more like Jonah than like Jesus, we better check our connection to the reservoir of the Holy Spirit!

Father, help us to live according to Your word in 1 Corinthians 13:6. Help us never to rejoice in injustice and always take joy in truth. Help us to flee evil and run rapidly toward integrity, justice, virtue, and righteousness. Thank You that You are conforming us to the image of Christ. Help us to hear the Holy Spirit guiding us to that end.

LOVE BEARS, BELIEVES, HOPES, AND ENDURES

It bears[G4722] all things, believes[G4100] all things, hopes[G1679] all things, endures[G5278] all things.

1 Corinthians 13:7

G4722 *stégō* – to cover. In the NT, to cover over in silence. (I) Generally meaning to conceal, with the accusative (1 Cor. 13:7, love hides the faults of others or covers them up). [27]

"**A**bove all, love one another deeply, because love covers over a multitude of sins" (1 Peter 4:8). If I love you, I am not thinking about the sins you have committed, and you are not thinking of mine. Love is the focus of both people above all. It is not that wrongs are swept under the rug but that they are covered by the blood of Jesus who died in our place. His love covered our sins and robed us in His righteousness. It is not my blood that covers their sins but the blood of Jesus. What right do I have to dredge up things Jesus already died for? Love minimizes the faults and flaws of others and praises the best in them.

G4100 *pisteúō* – to believe, have faith in, trust [28]

Love is trusting. I know, you may have been burned by someone you thought loved you. However, we must not throw doubt on everyone because of the wrong of one person. We need to believe the best of people while understanding that we all "have sinned and fall short of the glory of God" (Rom. 3:23). Ultimately our faith—belief— is in the Lord's ability to sustain our own and others' relationships with Him.

G1679 *elpízō* – to hope, expect with desire [29]

Love confidently hopes "what is good of another, even when others have ceased to hope".[31] Love is reluctant to think badly of someone and holds on to the hope that something that has the appearance of evil can be explained and proven to not be evil. Susan excels in this area. She had a friend whose behavior seemed to indicate to many of us that he might have dealt unscrupulously with her. However, she refused to believe ill of him even when circumstantial evidence seemed to prove his guilt. In the end, Susan was right to hope because our feelings about this person were incorrect. I (Susie) need to work on my skepticism and suspicion as I was one of his biggest detractors.

G5278 *hupŏmĕnō* – to remain under, i.e., to persevere, to endure, sustain, bear up under, suffer, as a load of miseries, adversities, persecutions or provocations with faith. [30]

Love patiently endures all things thrown at it, especially those adversities that come because of love for the Lord. Love does not give up. It perseveres. We have read many examples of this patient endurance in The Voice of the Martyrs publications and on their website www.persecution.com.

Father, help us to bear, believe, hope, and endure by the power of Your love flowing to us and through us.

LOVE NEVER FAILS

Love^{G26} never fails^{G1601}. But where there are prophecies, they will cease; where there are tongues, they will be restrained; where there is knowledge, it will be dismissed.

1 Corinthians 13:8

G1601 *ekpíptō* – Metaphorically to fall away, i.e., to fail, be without effect, to be in vain, love (1 Cor.13:8) [32]

G1601 *ekpíptō* – to drop away; specially, be driven out of one's course; figuratively, to lose, become inefficient: —be cast, fail, fall (away, off), take none effect. [33]

Prophecies, tongues, knowledge all will come to an end or no longer be needed. However, love never drops away, it has no end, it never fails. We really liked the picture that love cannot be driven off course. Love stays the course steadily. I (Susie) remember my parents talking about a conference they attended. The leader asked each person to describe their spouse in one word. My dad said my mom was "constant." What he meant by that is that her love was dependable, never changing, and consistent no matter what was going on in their lives or between them. Her love never failed, and they had been married fifty-four years when Jesus called

Daddy home. Love will pursue the best for someone. Put your name in there one more time. But this time, do it like this, "Susie's love never fails." I will fail, but I pray that my love for the Lord, His people, and those who need to be shown love to draw them to Him never fails.

How consistent is your love? Would people in your life describe you as someone they can constantly depend on to demonstrate love to them? Our love for others should not seem "on again, off again." It should be a golden thread of God's love woven throughout the tapestry of our lives.

Father, may our love never "wax cold" (Matt. 24:12). May we be people who persist in love and demonstrate Your love to everyone we encounter.

CRUCIFIED WITH CHRIST

When the Messiah was executed on the stake as a criminal, I was too; so that my proud ego no longer lives. But the Messiah lives in me, and the life I now live in my body I live by the same trusting faithfulness that the Son of God had, who loved^G25 *me and gave himself up for me.*

Galatians 2:20 (CJB)

The logo for Precious Jewels Ministries is designed to depict our three foundational scripture verses, one of which is Galatians 2:20 which in the King James Version begins, "I am crucified with Christ." If you look at our logo, you will see the letters PJM as if they are hanging on the cross. It is our way of visualizing that Christ nailed our sin to the cross thus crucifying our sin nature when we trusted totally in Him. What exactly does it mean in terms of our daily lives on this planet to be "crucified with Christ?" It means that we are no longer ego-centric (self-centered). We choose, instead to be Christ-centered and love selflessly. It means His Holy Spirit is working to make us more like Jesus every day, or as Paul put it, "to be conformed to the image of his Son" (Rom. 8:29). What does that look like? It involves exhibiting the Fruit of the Spirit found in Galatians 5:22-23, "But the fruit of the Spirit is love, joy, peace, patience, kindness, goodness, faithfulness, gentleness, and self-control. Against such things there is no law." Becoming Christ-like can only be achieved when the Holy Spirit lives in us. The Holy Spirit enters our lives when we trust completely in Jesus just as He trusted in and obeyed the Heavenly Father completely. We must let go of selfish ambitions and instead have "the mind of Christ" (Philippians 2:5) which means loving sacrificially as He did. We were crucified with Christ the moment we surrendered our lives to Him, but dying to self and living in Christ is a daily choice. Each day we must "take up our cross" (Matt. 16:24) and walk the path Jesus shows us. Yes, the logo advertises our ministry, but for us, it is a reminder to make that daily surrender to be "living sacrifices, holy, acceptable unto God, which is our reasonable service" (Rom. 12:1) and to love others as He loved us.

Take a moment to visualize yourself (ego, self-centeredness, sinful nature) hanging there on the cross with Jesus. Remember that if you have surrendered to Jesus, He now lives in and through you in the person of His Holy Spirit and enables you to exhibit the Fruit of the Spirit beginning with love.

Father, thank You for nailing our sin on the cross by sacrificing Your only begotten Son, Jesus. Thank You, that His death and resurrection enable us to be at peace with You, Holy God, and live daily as You would have us live. Help us to wake up each day with prais-

es on our lips and the determination to be complete-ly surrendered to Your will, to live as ones who have been forgiven and purchased with the blood of Jesus.

Phillips, Craig, and Dean have a beautiful song based on Galatians 2:20. You can listen to it here: https://www.youtube.com/watch?v=8T3EySH-o7w

THE DEPTH OF HIS LOVE

I ask that out of the riches of His glory He may strengthen you with power through His Spirit in your inner being, so that Christ may dwell in your hearts through faith. Then you, being rooted and grounded in love[G26], will have power, together with all the saints, to comprehend the length and width and height and depth of the love[G26] of Christ, and to know this love[G26] that surpasses knowledge, that you may be filled with all the fullness of God....

Ephesians 3:16-19

Paul knew how to pray for fellow believers. Notice he prayed that the Ephesians would be given the strength and competence to understand something that is beyond human ability to grasp—the love of Christ. We can only come to God's grace when His Spirit calls us, and we are only able to understand the depth of His love as He empowers us to do so. Then Paul prayed that they would be crammed full of God.

When I (Susie) was teaching middle school, I often prayed that God would give my students the ability to even begin understanding how much the Lord loved them. One day an illustration popped into my brain (wonder where it came from), and I asked my students to imagine themselves creating a Playdough™ world with people that would really come to life. They would be like a god to those people. I wove the story of their created world for a while and then asked them to imagine that the people ceased to believe they were real and taught their children that there were no such things as kindly giants that created them. I described a rebellion in Playdough™ world. Then I asked them if they would be willing to become a Playdough™ person and die for their rebellious creatures. Suddenly the light came on in a 6th grader's head, and he said, "Miss Hale! God created us from clay. We *are* the Playdough™ people, and Jesus *did* come into our world to die for us!" The room was silent for a moment as this truth sank in. I thought this would be the highlight of our week in Bible class. However, the next day we read the verses above. I asked the class if anyone could explain what they meant. A student raised his hand and said, "Isn't that what God did for us yesterday? He put that story in your head to help us all understand his love." What a teachable moment supplied by the grace of God! I know those students were being given a firm foundation of biblical truth, and I now pray that they are continuing to be filled with all God's Spirit has to offer them as many of them are raising children of their own.

My (Susan's) "aha moment" of understanding the magnitude of God's love for me came when I began elementary school in a pilot program of mainstreaming disabled children into the regular classroom. My wonderful first grade teacher's aide consistently demonstrated kindness, understanding, and love toward me. Instead of greeting me with "Good morning, Susan," she would say something like, "How's my sweetheart?" or "How's my darling this morning?" Before I even entered the classroom, I was feeling over ten feet tall because of the way she exemplified God's love to me. She was truly my "Jesus with skin on." I had surrendered my life to Jesus at the age of four. However, I lived in an extremely dysfunctional home. But when I went to school each day, God made sure I felt His love through the compassion of Mrs. M who helped school to be a place I could shine.

Heart check: Does the way you treat others consistently demonstrate God's love to them?

Father, help us to pray powerfully for fellow believers as Paul did. We pray the verses above for our family and friends and ourselves right now. Help us to grasp your love and be filled to the brim with your Spirit as was Susan's teacher's aide.

LOVINGLY EXPRESSING TRUTH

Instead, speaking the truth in love,[G26] we will in all things grow up into Christ Himself, who is the head.

Ephesians 4:15

Rather, let our lives lovingly[G26] express truth in all things – speaking truly, dealing truly, living truly. Enfolded in love,[G26] let us grow up in every way and in all things into Him, Who is the Head, [even] Christ, the Messiah, the Anointed One.

Ephesians 4:15 (AMPC)

We've heard the scripture "speaking the truth in love" quoted many times to justify blasting a sinking soul right out of the water. That may get him out of the sea and prevent him from sinking but picking up the shattered pieces afterward is a messy task for someone with the gift of mercy. We sometimes justify being blunt or harsh by saying our motivation is love. We've seen instances in which the stick of dynamite approach may be the only thing that will move someone. However, most of the time, we don't buy into destroying someone verbally as a means to the end of loving him into the kingdom of God.

Sticking with the sinking analogy, would it not be better to lovingly throw out a lifeline and gently pull the person in? The Amplified Classic version clarifies this verse well. We are to "lovingly express truth" not just in what we say but in our actions. "In love" describes not only why we speak the truth, but also how it is spoken. Truthfulness is supposed to help us all grow up into the image of Christ. I am only able to help my neighbor with loving truth when I have been truthful with myself, dealt truthfully with others, and lived God's truth out in my own life. Christ admonished us, "...first take the plank out of your own eye, and then you will see clearly to remove the speck from your brother's eye." (Matt. 7:5)

There are times when we need to remind a brother or sister of the truth in God's word and hope the reminder will pull them back out of the waves that can toss us about. But let us remember that we are all in the same boat, if you please. Next time I may be the one who has fallen overboard. I hope you'll try the life preserver on a strong line to pull me in before you go to the extreme of detonating a depth charge under me to propel me back into the boat. I hope I'll remember to do the same for you.

Father, help us to examine ourselves before examining others. Help us to discern when we are being judgmental rather than truly concerned for a brother or sister. Lord, help us to lovingly speak the truth in the context of living the truth and never use this verse as an excuse to deal harshly with a brother or sister.

WALKING IN DADDY'S LOVE

Be imitators of God, therefore, as beloved[G27] *children, and walk in love*[G26]*, just as Christ loved*[G25] *us and gave Himself up for us as a fragrant sacrificial offering to God.*

Ephesians 5:1-2

Therefore be imitators of God [copy Him and follow His example], as well-beloved children [imitate their father]. And walk in love, [esteeming and delighting in one another] as Christ loved us and gave Himself up for us, a slain offering and sacrifice to God [for you, so that it became] a sweet fragrance.

Ephesians 5:1-2 (AMPC)

G27 agapētós – from G25; beloved of God, means chosen by Him to salvation. [G40]

We are the beloved children of God our Father, meaning He chose us to be saved and become part of His forever family. We are to imitate Him and "walk in love". How many times have you watched a child imitate his or her parent? A little girl will try to put on make-up like Mom, or a child will stand on a chair or sit on the counter to help Mom cook. When I (Susan) was little, I had a toy phone. I would dial it and imitate

Mom's conversations, "Hello! This is Susan. What are you doing today? We need to go out to eat and the mall. I'll see you soon!" I also had a toy sink in my tub and would pretend to wash dishes. I didn't want to get out and would say, "I'm not finished yet. Please warm the water up again," because I liked doing my dishes! I (Susie) would "help" my dad mow the lawn or put oil in the car. Children imitate their parents.

How are we to imitate our Heavenly Father and His Son, Jesus? We are to be a "mini-me" of Jesus when it comes to love (and all the Fruit of the Spirit). We are to take delight in our brothers and sisters in Christ and enjoy each other. However, true Christian love often involves an element of sacrifice. True imitation of God is being willing to put another person's needs above our own. Christlikeness requires selflessness. We may not be called to literally die in someone's place as Jesus did for us, but we can die to our own selfishness in order to demonstrate His love to someone else. We have the ability to walk in love by the power of His Holy Spirit in us. But we have a choice each day as to whether we tap into the power of love or not. Christlikeness results in **JOY—J**esus first, **O**thers second, **Y**ourself last.

Father, help us to walk in love. Help us to be willing to put aside our own desires to fulfill someone else's need. Help us to be "Jesus with skin on" to someone who needs to feel Your love.

HUSBANDS' MISSION

Husbands, love[G25] *your wives, just as Christ loved*[G25]
the church and gave Himself up for her to sanctify her,
cleansing her by the washing with water through
the word, and to present her to Himself as a glorious
church, without stain or wrinkle or any such blemish,
but holy and blameless. In the same way, husbands
ought to love[G25] *their wives as their own bodies. He*
who loves[G25] *his wife loves*[G25] *himself.*

Ephesians 5:25-28

This passage may be familiar as it is used in weddings as well as sermons. To truly understand what Paul is writing to husbands, it is imperative to know the meaning of the Greek word for "love" used. Husbands are not commanded to love their wives in the sense of a romantic feeling because those feelings come and go and can be affected by situations. Husbands are not commanded to have the type love based on common interests and pursuits (*philĕō*) although they may be friends as well as husband and wife. They are instructed in Paul's letter, commanded by the Lord, to love (*agapáō*) their wives. Remember that agapáō is the willful choice to love whether or not the object of that love is worthy at the time. *Agapáō* is self-sacrificing love that puts the needs of the other person above his own. Husbands, as the leaders of their homes, are given the mission to love as Christ loved. Christ died in order to purify His bride, the church. The husband's goal is to love his wife remembering that she is God's precious, priceless jewel entrusted to her husband's care while on earth. He should never belittle his wife or cause her to stumble in her walk with the Lord. He should help her to shine as the multi-faceted diamond God intends her to become. Since the husband and wife become "one flesh," he should love her, take care of her, as he would take care of himself. All of this is predicated on the home where both husband and wife are believers—children of God—because it is impossible to love in this manner without the indwelling of the Holy Spirit.

Susan and I do not have husbands but submit to the Lord as our head. However, since we share a home, we should love (*agapáō*) each other. Married or single, we should ask ourselves if our homes are a picture of God's love. This passage is written to husbands, but the principle of loving as Christ loves applies in all relationships between believers as well.

Father, may our homes reflect You not only by having scripture on the walls and other Christian décor but in the love, joy, peace, patience, kindness, gentleness, goodness, faithfulness, and self-control found in the people who dwell there.

ABOUNDING IN AGÁPĒ

And this is my prayer: that your love^{G26} may abound
more and more in knowledge and depth of insight, so
that you may be able to test and prove what is best
and may be pure and blameless for the day of Christ,
filled with the fruit of righteousness that comes
through Jesus Christ, to the glory and praise of God.

Philippians 1:9-11

Biblical love is not stagnant. The Holy Spirit is growing the love of Jesus in and through believers as we gain knowledge of the word of God and develop discernment. Paul prays that the Philippians' love (agápē) will "abound more and more in knowledge and depth of insight." What exactly does that mean? We went to one of our favorite resources to increase our understanding:

> **Knowledge -** This is from the Gr. word that describes genuine, full, or advanced knowledge. Biblical love is not an empty sentimentalism but is anchored deeply in the truth of Scripture and regulated by it (cf. Eph. 5:2, 3; 1 Pet. 1:22, 1 Peter 1:22 ESV). [41]

Love discerns what is best for someone rather than just gushing emotion on them. Love cares enough to lovingly speak truth to a fellow believer when needed. Love is also the Fruit of the Spirit from which all the other fruit stems. As our relationship with Christ grows, our love grows; and as our love of Christ grows, our relationship with Him deepens. It is cyclical. Love that grows in knowledge and insight is a journey toward maturity rather than love being a one-time destination.

Have you reached a place where your love for Jesus and others seems stagnant? Pray Paul's prayer above for yourself. Is there someone in your life who is just beginning their journey with Jesus? Pray this prayer for him or her.

Father, may we never become stagnant in our walk with You or in our love for the body of Christ—the Messianic Community. Help us to abound in love that is genuine and consistent with Your word.

LIKE-MINDED LOVE

Therefore if you have encouragement in Christ, if any comfort from His love[G26], if any fellowship with the Spirit, if any affection and compassion, then make my joy complete by being like-minded, having the same love[G26], being *__united in spirit__ and purpose. Do nothing out of selfish ambition or empty pride, but in humility **__consider others more important than yourselves__. Each of you should look not only to your own interests, but also to the interests of others.

Philippians 2:1-4

> ***one accord**. This may also be translated "united in spirit" and perhaps is a term specially coined by Paul. It lit. means "one-souled" and describes people who are knit together in harmony, having the same desires, passions, and ambitions. ****_esteem others better than himself._** The basic definition of true humility (cf. Rom. 12:10; Gal. 5:13; Eph. 5:21; 1 Pet. 5:5). [42]

If we are in fellowship with the Spirit of Christ, we will become steadily more like Him— ... "conformed to the image of His son" (Rom. 8:29). The first evidence of this transformation is "being like-minded, having the same love, being united in spirit and purpose". The evidence that we are His disciples is that we love one another (John 13:35). We are to be united in spirit which can be interpreted as "one-souled". Susan and I feel our souls have been knit together by God with the result that we are as close or closer than biological sisters. Paul's desire was that all believers develop and demonstrate this kind of bond. We are to have the humility in love to consistently think of others before ourselves. Christ was, of course, the perfect example of this humility. Continue reading in Philippians chapter two, and you will see exactly how much Jesus put us before Himself. He came to earth as a humble baby, ministered to all kinds of people, and obeyed His Father to the point of suffering a humiliating death on the cross. But don't stop reading at verse eight. Go on to read how God has exalted Jesus and how *everyone* will *eventually* bow to Him (Philippians 2:9-11).

If the Son of God could love unlovable sinners such as ourselves, surely, we can love each other. If the Lord of Heaven and Earth could demonstrate such humility in order to serve and save us, surely, we can put our own needs aside to serve others that He loves. Time for a heart check. Examine yourself to see how well you are living up to the attitudes and actions Paul told the Philippians would bring him joy. Not only will these Christ-like behaviors bring us joy, but they would also be well-pleasing to God our Father.

Father, help us to exemplify the love of Jesus for all the people You place in our paths.

Therefore, as the elect of God, holy and beloved[G25], clothe yourselves with hearts of compassion, kindness, humility, gentleness, and patience. Bear with one another and forgive any complaint you may have against someone else. Forgive as the Lord forgave you. And over all these virtues put on love[G26], which is the bond of perfect unity.

Colossian 3:12-14

CLOTHE ME IN CHRIST'S VIRTUES

Lord, cover me with compassion,
enrobe me with your kindness.
As people look upon my life,
I pray Your beauty they will see.

Allow me to walk humbly
exhibiting gentleness and patience.
Please clothe me in Christ's virtues
to be all that I should be.

Lord, help me to be forbearing,
Freely forgiving others
Just as You in Your kindness
Have freely forgiven me.

Above all of these traits, Lord,
Help me to put on Your love,
For love is the glue that binds
All these virtues perfectly.

OVERWHELMING, OVERFLOWING LOVE

And may the Lord cause you to increase and over-flow with love for one another and for everyone else, just as our love for you overflows . . .
                                        1 Thessalonians 3:12

May the Lord flood you with an unending, undying love for one another and for all humanity, like our love for you
                              1 Thessalonians 3:12 (VOICE)

G4052 -*perisseúō*, per-is-syoo'-o; from G4053; to superabound (in quantity or quality), be in excess, be superfluous; also (transitively) to cause to super-abound or excel:—(make, more) abound, (have, have more) abundance (be more) abundant, be the better, enough and to spare, exceed, excel, increase, be left, redound, remain (over and above).(44)

Exponential Love: Paul's insistence on love as the chief characteristic that defines the church's fel-lowship is clearly portrayed here. Note the words translated "increase" and "abound" (1 Thess. 3:12). The Greek words are pleonazō and peris-seuō respectively. Both terms carry the idea of su-pra-abundance; that is, having more than enough, a running over. Using both words may seem to be redundant, but it is Paul's way of emphasizing the fact that believers should love one another. [45]

Every positive attribute the Christian exhibits begins with the Lord and circles back to Him. He is the one who endows us, floods us, drowns us in His perfect love, thus enabling us to love one another within the body of Christ. Then this love superabounds, over-flows, grows exponentially enabling us to share the love of Jesus with non-believers—"everyone else" or "all humanity"—as well as toward our brothers and sisters in Christ.

Remember: This type of love is not a gush of emotion or warm fuzzy feeling. It is a deliberate choice of the will to demonstrate the love of God to others. It is be-stowing compassion regardless of the other person's deservedness or reaction—to love whether the person is "lovely" or seems "loveable" or not. Recall studying exponents in mathematics. If you have 2^{10} (two to the tenth power), it is 2x2x2x2x2x2x2x2x2x2=1024. Paul prayed that God would grow our Christ-like love ex-ponentially! Pray to have this overflowing love. Pray this for your biological and spiritual children. As the song says, "They will know we are Christians by our love." Listen to it here: https://www.youtube.com/watch?v=3EBShVUTHoU

Father, please cause our love for Your "framily" to overflow and superabound to show love to non-believers in order to point them to You, the Source of our love.

CLOTHED IN CHRISTLIKENESS

Therefore, as the elect of God, holy and beloved, clothe yourselves with hearts of compassion, kindness, humility, gentleness, and patience. Bear with one another and forgive any complaint you may have against someone else. Forgive as the Lord forgave you. And over all these virtues put on love,[G26] which is the bond of perfect unity.
Colossians 3:12-14

Recently, we saw some women from India wearing gorgeous, silken saris. They were completely wrapped in luxurious cloth, literally clothed in beauty. We are to be clothed in the virtues of Jesus Christ. Just as we consciously put on the armor of the Lord (Ephesians 6) each morning, we should also don compassion, kindness, humility, gentleness, and patience. This cannot be done in our own strength. We must walk closely with the Lord and allow him to enrobe us in His righteousness. We are to forgive as the Lord forgave us. Quite a statement. He forgave us completely on the cross even though we were not deserving and had not yet asked for forgiveness. He did not wait for us to earn His forgiveness in any way, shape, or form. Nor should we demand a changed life of our brothers and sisters before we extend forgiveness.

Paul uses the same verb translated "clothe" in verse 12 for "put on" in verse 14. Remember the saris the women were wearing?

sari – sari, also spelled saree, principal outer garment of women of the Indian subcontinent, consisting of a piece of often brightly coloured, frequently embroidered, silk, cotton, or, in recent years, synthetic cloth five to seven yards long. It is worn wrapped around the body with the end left hanging or used over the head as a hood.(43)

Love is to be our beautiful, elegant sari, worn over all the other virtues of Christ. The love of Christ emanating from us will catch the eye of many who need to know him as those saris caught our eyes. Allow Jesus's love to flow from you like the beautifully flowing silk of a sari, and He will draw people into His family through you.

List some loving actions to be woven into your "sari" of Jesus's love. We'll start you out with listening to or praying for a friend, helping a neighbor, sending an encouragement note . . .

Father, help us to be clothed in the righteousness of Christ each day. Help us to be compassionate, kind, humble, gentle, and patient with our co-workers, family, friends, and especially those who need to see You in us. Help us to forgive others as Jesus forgave us and help us to be draped in the beauty of your love.

EXEMPLIFYING CHRIST-LIKE LOVE

Let no one despise your youth, but set an example for the believers in speech, in conduct, in love[G26]*, in faith, in purity.*

1 Timothy 4:12

Love in the context of the verse above is Christ-like love. It is a choice to love rather than being based on an emotional response. Paul was exhorting Timothy that even though he was relatively young to be a pastor, he could be a model of the kind of love shown by the God-Man Jesus, the Christian kind of love. Paul the Apostle placed Timothy in the position of overseer—pastor—to the believers in Ephesus and must have felt he was equipped for that challenge despite his youth. Paul encouraged Timothy to be exemplary in all facets of biblical godliness. He was to sparkle as one of God's precious jewels among the believers.

I have a dear friend who is a prime example of this type of love, truly a precious jewel. Janelle had already shown me love in many ways when she came to visit me saying, "I have to apologize to you." Incredulously I asked, "Why would you need to apologize to me?" She explained that she had loved me but not as Christ would love me. She said Jesus had asked her specifically to love me as He would, on His behalf, and she had answered "yes." She has fulfilled that promise to the Lord many times over. She stayed with me in the hospital in Tulsa to give my family members an opportunity to rest and freshen up. She visited me numerous times in my apartment. Janelle even flew all the way from Arkansas to Texas to stay with me in the hospital while Susie went to prepare a place for me in her home—now *our* home—since the Lord had knit us together as sisters. Janelle met my needs with a tender care that can only come from the love of Jesus within her. When she sees me, she sees Jesus and ministers to me as if I were He. Her Christlike love is an example of how the "familyship" of God should behave toward one another.

Do you have a Janelle in your life? Better yet, are you being that kind of loving, consistent friend to a sister or brother? Pray the Lord will surround and fill you with this agápē love.

Father, fill us with agápē, the love for "framily" and even the unlovely, going out of our way to demonstrate grace, love, and kindness to everyone.

PURSUE LOVE

But you, O man of God, flee from these things and pursue righteousness, godliness, faith, love[G26], perseverance, and gentleness.

1 Timothy 6:11

The man of God, Timothy, needed to run from false teaching and the sin that accompanied it and follow after, pursue the things in keeping with the word of God. One thing he was to run after was love. Not erotic, emotional love or even that of strong friendship, but unconditional, Christ-like love. In order to do this, he must stay in the word of God, not just to read it but to live it out, to walk in it. Believers walk in the word by every decision that is in keeping with the scripture. To walk in this "agápē" love begins with a fervent love for the Lord which then extends to the love of others (Matt. 22:37-39). We do not sit around waiting for an opportunity to present itself to us in order to show God's love. We must hunt down and chase after opportunities to love.

I (Susan) had a pastor/mentor/father-in-the-faith who consistently pursued love. My former pastor, Doug, loved the Lord Jesus and proclaimed His gospel faithfully. He has shown me love during many crisis times in my life. He has tracked me down like a hunter at various hospitals to pray with me and show me the love of God. Knowing that he stood behind me in my pursuit of God and was instrumental in my ordination encouraged me greatly. He even said that signing my ordination papers was one of the greatest pleasures of his life. He loved me at that pinnacle of my life, and he loved me when I was cut down (literally pruned!). God has used Doug's faithful, Christlike love to hold me up in times of trial. Doug White is now with the Savior whose love consistently flowed through him, and I'm sure he still celebrates me from above.

Do you have a Doug in your life? Thank the Lord for that person and lift them up in prayer. Are you steadfast in your love for a brother or sister in the Lord? Is there someone the Lord is nudging you to pursue in order to show them His love?

Lord of Love, instill in us the ability and desire to pursue love in Your name. Thank You for the loving brothers and sisters in Christ who have relentlessly loved us by being Your loving arms enfolding us in so many ways.

LOVE IS AN ACTION WORD

*Flee from youthful passions and pursue righteousness,
faith, love[G26], and peace, together with those who call
on the Lord out of a pure heart.*

2 Timothy 2:22

Rather than embracing erotic love, physical pleasures, gluttonous appetites, and miserly wealth,
Paul instructed Timothy to run after Christlike, self-sacrificing love. As a pastor, one should embrace the prin-
ciples that Christ embodied. A pastor should be eager
to visit those in hospitals, the bereaved, and those in
prison. He/she should reach out to those members in
nursing homes or home-found (not home-bound because they are not chained there, but you find them
there—It's a "Susanism"). Paul gave Timothy explicit
instructions considering widows, but today that might
include single parents or grandparents caring for their
grandchildren. The pastor may not be able to personally
minister to each member of the congregation, but he or
she should encourage a plan for others to do so. A pastor
may, of necessity, delegate these responsibilities. However, he or she needs to lead workers to lovingly minister
to those in need. The agápē principle is that we choose
to love. It is a love that springs from the heart of God
and is relentless and passionate whether our emotions

are involved or not. It is *not* so much loving *because* as it is loving *despite*—loving whether the recipient of the love seems worthy or even appreciative or not. No matter what their response is, the godly person continues to demonstrate God's love. This kind of love comes from an eternal rather than a temporal perspective. Not only paid pastors are called to demonstrate this kind of love. All of us as believers are called to share the love of Jesus with everyone within our circle of influence.

Brainstorm specific ways you can spread the love of Jesus with people you know. If you have children, plan ways to include them in loving deeds to teach them that love is an action word.

Father, infuse us with Your love to the point that we cannot help but let it bubble over effervescently onto others. Help us to love the unlovely exuberantly. Help us to be more like Jesus in loving!

REPUTATION FOR FAITH AND LOVE

I always thank my God, remembering you in my prayers, because I hear about your faith in the Lord Jesus and your love[G26] for all the saints.

Philemon 1:4-5

After greeting Philemon and others with him, Paul let him know that he prayed for him and thanked God that he had a reputation for faith in the Lord and love for the saints. What an encouragement that must have been to Philemon! Are you and I people that cause others to thank God as they pray for us? Are we known for our faith and love? I hope so. It's something to meditate on, to think of how other people might remember us as they pray. Are they thanking the Lord for us or asking Him to make us aware of areas that we need to surrender to Him? This may help us to realize some things in our lives might need to change. We may need to rely more on the Lord and be more demonstrative in our love for our brothers and sisters in Christ. Another thought came to mind as I read this. How often do I encourage other believers by letting them know how God has used them in my life or how I've observed Him using them to bless others? Do I commend my friends when they demonstrate faith in Christ? Do I pray for God to strengthen them and me in these areas?

There are many people in my life that I should send a card or letter to in order to encourage them as they have encouraged me. Perhaps I should take some time this weekend to follow through on that idea. Do you need to do the same? Ask the Lord to bring those people to mind that you need to pray for, thank the Lord for, and encourage by sending a card or email or maybe calling them on the phone. This is an excellent way to demonstrate our love for the "familyship" of God.

Father, seeing others rely upon You strengthens our own faith. Thank You for the positive examples of faith and love You have given us through many believers over the years. Help us to take the time to write some notes this weekend. Help us also to be an example of faithfulness and love to others.

SINCERE LOVE FROM SANCTIFIED HEARTS

Since you have purified your souls by obedience to the truth so that you have a genuine love^{G5360} for your brothers, love^{G25} one another deeply, from a pure heart.

1 Peter 1:22

Since by your obedience to the truth you have purified yourselves for a sincere love of the believers, [see that you] love one another from the heart [always unselfishly seeking the best for one another]

1 Peter 1:22 (AMP)

The blood of Jesus washes us clean because of His sacrifice on the cross. However, if you love the Lord, the Holy Spirt is continually sanctifying you to make you more like Christ. There is no benefit to reading the word of God, the truth, unless one obeys what has been learned. That obedience by the power of the Spirit within us makes us pure. We cannot love "from a pure heart" if we are not cooperating in our purification by obeying God's word, not because of compulsion or obligation, but because of our love for and relationship with Jesus. Then the Holy Spirit will grow in us authentic, fervent love for the family of God, our brothers and sisters in Christ. We often end a letter by signing love and our name. We say good-bye on the phone with a quick, "Love you." Are these just greetings we use because of tradition and habit or do we sincerely, deeply love our brothers and sisters in Christ?

As we have stated in previous devotions, love is an action word. It can be a noun, but it is also a verb. How are you demonstrating your love in the family of God? It could be listening to a brother or sister as they walk through difficult circumstances. It could be by meeting the needs of a "framily" member when times are tough. It could be as simple as a phone call or text to check on a church member who has missed Sunday school a couple of times. Ask the Lord to show you ways to demonstrate your love for His family. Then put that sincere love into action this week in whatever ways God leads you.

Father, by Your Holy Spirit enable us to understand and obey Your word. May our response to the Spirit's prompting be eager and earnest obedience. Develop in us Christlike love for Your forever family and show us how to put that love into action.

ADONAI'S ADDITION

For this very reason, make every effort to add to your faith virtue; and to virtue, knowledge; and to knowledge, self-control; and to self-control, perseverance; and to perseverance, godliness; and to godliness, brotherly kindness; and to brotherly kindness, love[G26]. For if you possess these qualities and continue to grow in them, they will keep you from being ineffective and unproductive in your knowledge of our Lord Jesus Christ. But whoever lacks these traits is nearsighted to the point of blindness, having forgotten that he has been cleansed from his past sins.

2 Peter 1:5-9

But the fruit of the Spirit is love[G26], joy, peace, patience, kindness, goodness, faithfulness, gentleness, and self-control. Against such things there is no law.

Galatians 5:22-23

Notice the overlap between what Paul is teaching us in Galatians 5:22-23 (The Fruit of the Spirit) and what Peter teaches in 2 Peter 1:5-9. Paul begins with love, and Peter ends with love. Love forms the bookends for all the traits the Holy Spirit develops in believers. God is love (1 John 4:8). He is also the alpha and omega (Revelation 1:8) which represents the beginning and the end. Love begins with the Almighty God loving us to the utmost by sending His Son to die in our place. As we surrender to His love for us, He enables us to love Him and then to love others. "We love because He first loved us" (1 John 4:19). From that Christlike love flows all the Fruit of the Spirit and all the character traits Peter urges us to add one upon another. Adonai (literally my Lord) through both Paul and Peter emphasizes that these traits build on each other. When you add up the Fruit of the Spirit and Peter's list of traits, the sum is Christlikeness. God enables us to move toward this goal by the power of His Holy Spirit within us, and ultimately, we will be completely sanctified (made holy). "His divine power has given us everything we need to experience life and to reflect God's true nature through the knowledge of the One who called us by His glory and virtue" (2 Peter 1:3 VOICE).

Our capacity to be holy as He is holy (1 Peter 1:16) is only limited by how much we tap into the Holy Spirit by increasing our knowledge of and devotion to the Lord Jesus and surrender to God's will. As we obey what God has shown us in His word, we become more like the Lord. Do you see the Fruit of the Spirit developing in your life through the addition of Christlike traits? Ask the Lord to let His Spirit flow through you that others may see Jesus in you. Your life may be the only living reflection of Jesus someone may experience. Make it count!

Father, we ask You to keep adding Christlikeness to our characters that others will see Jesus reflected in our lives. May our demeanors be as much of a witness for Christ as our words.

DISTINGUISHED BY RIGHTEOUSNESS AND LOVE

By this the children of God are distinguished from the children of the devil: Anyone who does not practice righteousness^{G1343} is not of God, nor is anyone who does not love^{G25} his brother. This is the message you have heard from the beginning: We should love^{G25} one another.

1 John 3:10-11

> G1343 *dikaiosýnē* – . . . denotes the state acceptable to God which becomes a sinner's possession through that faith by which he embraces the grace of God offered him in the expiatory death of Jesus Christ . . . (46)

Believers are credited with the righteousness of Christ the moment we surrender our lives to Him. However, we are also commanded to "*practice* righteousness" on a day-to-day basis. This requires a moment-by-moment surrender to that righteousness the Holy Spirit is working within us. We cannot, in our own power, develop a right relationship with a Holy God. Our righteousness is born of our relationship with Jesus. The way we live our lives, how we interact with others, is an outward demonstration of the inward change God has made and is continually making in us. Our love for our brothers and sisters in Christ is another evidence that we belong to God. This love is a choice, an act of our will, to love those in the family of God. John here is reiterating his quote of Jesus in John 13:35, "By this everyone will know that you are My disciples, if you love one another." Our ability to be righteous and to love others stems from being born into the family of God. Religion and ritual without relationship is dead.

Do you find yourself striving and struggling to be obedient to what you know of the Bible? Are you trying to obey God's word without having a relationship with the Word made flesh? Do a heart check. We cannot *do* the deeds of God unless we *are* children of God. If you have never surrendered your life to Jesus, acknowledged His right to your entire being, that is where you must begin. If you have been blessed to be walking with the Lord already, ask His holy Spirit to love others through you and guide you in the path of righteousness. That is a prayer He will answer.

Father, help us to never be so haughty as to think we can be righteous apart from Jesus. Help us to humbly pursue the practice of daily righteousness leaning on the power of the Holy Spirit within us. May Your love for Your children flow through us to our brothers and sisters in Christ.

LOVE IN ACTION AND TRUTH

By this we know what love^G26 is: Jesus laid down His life for us, and we ought^G3784 to lay down our lives for our brothers. If anyone with earthly possessions sees his brother in need, but withholds his compassion from him, how can the love^G26 of God abide in him? Little children, let us love^G25 not in word and speech, but in action and truth.

1 John 3:16-18

G3784 *opheílō* – Metaphorically, to be bound or obligated to perform a duty, meaning I ought, must . . . [47]

1 John 3:16 - **He laid down His life for us.** This expression is unique to John (John 10:11, 15, 17, 18; 13:37, 38; 15:13) and speaks of divesting oneself of something. Christian love is self-sacrificing and giving. Christ's giving up His life for believers epitomized the true nature of Christian love (John 15:12, 13; Phil. 2:5–8; 1 Pet. 2:19–23). **we also ought to lay down our lives for the brethren.** God calls Christians to that same standard of love for one another as He had for us (see v. 16a). [48]

Jesus literally laid down His life for us when He died on the cross in our place. We are obligated as believers to exhibit this same kind of love toward our brothers and sisters in Christ. We may not be called to literally die in someone's place, but our love should be exponentially self-sacrificing, always preferring others by putting their needs above our own. This is the standard of Christian love. We are to be servants rather than to be served above all else. The example given is that if we have means we should help those less fortunate than ourselves. It has been our experience that even brothers or sisters in Christ who have very little give freely to those who have less than themselves. There is no place for selfishness in God's economy. We are to take care of one another. John sums it up by explaining that mere lip service won't cut it, we are to love "in action and truth." Over and over, as we have studied the Fruit of the Spirit "love," we have found that it is a verb, an action word. There is a saying, "Put your money where your mouth is." John is saying your actions should demonstrate the love you claim to have with your mouth. "Suppose a brother or sister is without clothes and daily food. If one of you tells him, "Go in peace; stay warm and well fed," but does not provide for his physical needs, what good is that?" (James 2:15-16). James was talking about faith without works, but love without action is just as empty and useless.

Sincere love is demonstrated in how we treat others. Are you being the hands and feet of Jesus by showing your love to others through compassionate actions?

Father, help our deeds back up our words of love. Help us to be a blessing to others and to share what we have generously.

G25 – *agapáō* – To esteem, love, indicating a direction of the will and finding one's joy in something or someone.[49]

LOVE ONE ANOTHER

We are commanded to love one another
Over and over and over again.
This love is different than the love of a brother
and not the love usually found among men.
The love we are commanded to show
Is a choice to love, an act of the will.
It's the kind of love our Lord bestows—
Even though we sin, He loves us still.
We must choose to treat others with respect,
to show love though it's undeserved.
We do for them what they would not expect.
We *choose* to love and *choose* to serve.
Jesus chose to love those who killed Him
And even forgave them from the cross.
We are to pray for and love our enemies,
Even those who have caused us great loss.
This kind love is not based in emotion,
For emotions change from day to day.
This is a *choice* of steadfast love
No matter what obstacles come our way.

GOD IS LOVE

Beloved^(G27), let us love^(G25) one another, because love^(G26) comes from God. Everyone who loves^(G25) has been born of God and knows God. Whoever does not love^(G25) does not know God, because God is love^(G26).

1 John 4:7-8

> G27 *agapētós* - . . . beloved of God, means chosen by Him to salvation [(50)]

In these verses, the Apostle John is addressing believers, those chosen by God to be saved, those in the family of God. This is obvious not only because he addresses them as "beloved" but because, as we have learned previously, only those born again in Christ are capable of this type of love. He reiterates that concept by stating plainly, "Everyone who loves (*agapáō*) has been born of God and knows God." This willingly sacrificial Christlike love is what sets believers apart from the world. It is a selfless love meaning that the believer is seeking what he or she can do for others rather than having his or her own needs met. It is how people know that we belong to Jesus (John 13:35). Keep in mind that non-believers are capable of other kinds of love but not agápē. In our fallen state, before we surrender our lives to Christ and receive His gift of salvation, we are incapable of this kind of love. That is why John says that those who do not love (agápē), do not know God. God *is* love. When we become a part of His family—when we truly know Him—He enables us through the Holy Spirit within us, to love as He loves. Love envelopes us and flows through us because of our intimate relationship with our Lord Jesus Christ. At the point that we receive Christ, we have the capacity to love in this way. However, love develops in us as we grow in that relationship with Jesus. As we mature, we are more *consistent* in choosing to love selflessly.

We are not to judge others based on our perception of their love capacity. We must always be examining *our own* hearts. How well do we measure up to loving others as Jesus loved them? Do we recognize a need to grow in Christ-like love? Are we putting into practice the things we have learned about the kind of love we are to have for one another?

Father, thank You for loving us unconditionally and saving us by Your grace. Help us to be gracious and love our brothers and sisters in Christ selflessly.

GOD'S LOVE REVEALED

This is how God's love[G26] was revealed among us:
God sent His one and only Son into the world, so that
we might live through Him. And love[G26] consists in
this: not that we loved[G25] God, but that He loved[G25] us
and sent His Son as the atoning sacrifice for our sins.

1 John 4:9-10

God *is* love. How has God revealed His love to humankind? God sent Jesus to be born miraculously through the virgin Mary, to walk on earth and experience everything we humans do but without sinning, to preach and teach about the Father's love for us, and then to *die* upon the cross in our place to satisfy God's wrath toward our sin. The emphasis is *not* our love for God but *His* love for us. When Jesus died, He paid the price for our sin and redeemed us from the certain destination of Hell—separation from God and all that is good forever. Jesus made it possible for us to truly live while on earth— to live with hope rather than defeat, to live abundantly (John 10:10). When God raised Jesus from the dead on the third day, He opened the pathway for all who trust in Him to look forward to bodily resurrection from death and then to live eternally with Him in a perfect world. Jesus's love for us continues as He prepares a place for us to live forever (John 14) and as He is ever interceding for us: "For Christ Jesus, who died, and more than that was raised to life, is at the right hand of God—and He is interceding for us" (Romans 8:34b).

God loves us. God loves *you*. Let that truth sink in for a moment. In light of that truth, may we be energized to love others as He has commanded. God chose to reveal His love for us through the person of His Son, the God-Man: "The Son is the radiance of God's glory and the exact representation of His nature, upholding all things by His powerful word" (Hebrews 1:3a). Jesus Christ was the one and only acceptable sacrifice, God's spotless Lamb. No further sacrifices are needed because Jesus paid the entire debt. We have received an immeasurable gift—salvation by grace—because of God's love demonstrated by the death and resurrection of Jesus. How selfish would it be to keep this Good News to ourselves? The most loving thing we can do for those who do not yet know Jesus is to tell them about God's love and how He has changed our lives.

Father, as we are reminded of the depth of Your love, let us be inspired to share that love not only in words but through our deeds. Let others see Your love in our changed lives and in how we treat other people. Let our lives be consistent with our testimony of Your love and grace.

WE OUGHT TO LOVE

Beloved^{G27}, if God so loved^{G25} us, we also ought^{G3784} to love^{G25} one another.

1 John 4:11

> G3784 *opheílō* – Metaphorically, to be bound or obligated to perform a duty, meaning I ought, must . . . [51]

In the previous devotional, we looked at exactly how God demonstrated His love for us by sending His own Son to die in our place. The Father sacrificed His only Son born of the virgin Mary. Jesus was not God's adopted child like we are. The Holy Spirit miraculously placed Jesus in the womb of a human woman without benefit of a human male. God, out of His perfect love for us, gave His most precious Son to pay the debt we owed. Therefore, we "ought"—we are obligated—to love one another.

> **4:11** God's sending His Son gives Christians not only salvation privilege, but obligation to follow this pattern of sacrificial love. Christian love must be self-sacrificing like God's love. [52]

In previous devotionals, we have seen that God revealed His love to us, Jesus commanded us to love, and we are to love in action and truth. Now we find that we are *obligated* to love. It is our duty as children of God to love others in the way He has loved us. As children we sang, "I'm in the Lord's army!" Soldiers have duties they are obligated to perform. As soldiers in the Lord's army, we are obligated to fulfill our duty to love one another. Are we excellent soldiers?

Father, may we serve You with gladness and enter Your courts with praise (Psalm 100:4). May we, as obedient children and good soldiers, fulfill our duty to love others as You have loved us.

LOVE PERFECTED

No one has ever seen God; but if we love^{G25} one anoth-er, God remains in us, and His love^{G26} is perfected^{G5048} in us.

1 John 4:12

G5048 *teleióō* – (II) Metaphorically meaning to make perfect although not faultless but bringing to a state of com-pletion or fulfillment.

(A) Generally (John 17:23, "that they may be [perfect or completely unit-ed in] on'" 2 Cor. 12:9, "My power shows itself perfect in weakness" [a.t.]. meaning that it appears as a need arises; James 2:22, 1 John 2:5; 4:12, 17, 18). [53]

"**G**od remains in us." Because we are indwelt by the Holy Spirit of God, we are enabled to love as He loved. His power overcomes our weakness at the moment we need it so that others see His love through us.

Philippians 2:13 (AMP) For it is [not your strength, but it is] God who is ef-fectively at work in you, both to will and

> *to work [that is, strengthening, energiz-*
> *ing, and creating in you the longing and*
> *the ability to fulfill your purpose] for His*
> *good pleasure.*

God's love is made perfect—mature—in us not through our striving but by His power at work in our lives. This side of Heaven, we will never love perfectly uncondi- tionally as the Lord does. However, He is maturing us as we follow Him day-by-day. Love is maturing in us like a seed matures into a plant. God placed a seed of His love in us the moment we received Christ. We water it with God's word and bathe it in the "Sonlight" by prayer and praise. This seed will continue to grow into a flourishing plant because God is the master gardener!

> *Philippians 1:6 He who began a good*
> *work in you will carry it on to comple-*
> *tion until the day of Christ Jesus.*

Are you doing your part to grow the seed of love God placed within you? Are you reading the Bible to water it, and keeping your focus on Jesus as the Light by prayer and praise? (Hebrews 12:2).

Father, help us to do our part in growing Your love by studying the Bible, spending time in prayer, and being obedient to Your command to love. We trust that what you have called us to do, You will empower us to do. Thank You for infusing us with Your strength and Your love.

Jesus declared, "'Love^G25 the Lord your God with all your heart and with all your soul and with all your mind.' This is the first and greatest commandment. And the second is like it: 'Love^G25 your neighbor as yourself.' All the Law and the Prophets hang on these two commandments."

Matthew 22:37-40

And you shall love^157 the LORD your God with all your heart and with all your soul and with all your strength.

Deuteronomy 6:5

Do not seek revenge or bear a grudge against any of your people, but love^H157 your neighbor as yourself. I am the LORD.

Leviticus 19:18

PERPETUAL, HABITUAL, INTENTIONAL LOVE

God's love for us is never-ending,
Never-changing, and perpetual.
God's love for His chosen children
lasts forever and is unconditional.
Love is proven by our obedience
But cannot be reduced to mere ritual.

The commands of God are not just rules.
The Ten Commandments are relational:
Relationships with our Lord and others,
How to live lovingly with individuals.
Our love for our brothers and sisters
Should be consistent and habitual.
Our Christ-like love for others
Must always be intentional.

ABIDING IN LOVE

If anyone confesses that Jesus is the Son of God, God abides in him, and he in God. And we have come to know and believe the love[G26] *that God has for us. God is love*[G26]*; whoever abides in love*[G26] *abides in God, and God in him. In this way, love*[G26] *has been perfected among us, so that we may have confidence on the day of judgment; for in this world we are just like Him.*

1 John 4:15-17

To them God has chosen to make known among the Gentiles the glorious riches of this mystery, which is Christ in you, the hope of glory.

Colossians 1:27

4:16b The Old Testament Israelite would look with wonder at the tabernacle or temple because the presence of God was in that building. No person, besides the high priest once a year, would dare to enter the Holy of Holies, where God was enthroned in glory. But we have God's Spirit living in us! We abide in this love, and we experience the abiding of God in us. [54]

When we surrender our lives to Christ, when we profess our faith in Him as the Son of God, His Holy Spirit comes to live in us as the pledge or assurance of our inheritance (Ephesians 1:14). Our bodies become the temple of God (1 Corinthians 6:19). We experience the love of God, and that love fills us. Therefore, we "abide" or live in God's love, and we live in God as He lives in us. In His high priestly prayer, Jesus asked the Father to make believers united as one with Him and each other—to become the family of God. In this way, believers would be made perfect or mature and by our love, the world would be shown the love of God.

> *John 17:22-23 I have given them the glory You gave Me, so that they may be one as We are one—I in them and You in Me—that they may be perfectly united, so that the world may know that You sent Me and have loved them just as You have loved Me.*

This is the question we must ask ourselves: "Is the fact that we are abiding in God's love clearly evident to those around us? Do our lives proclaim God's love?" We *are* abiding in God's love by His grace; but as we have said before, we need to tap into the power given to us by the Holy Spirit to consistently radiate the love of our Father to each other and the world. We are to reflect His love as His multifaceted, precious jewels.

Father, we are blessed to abide in Your love and have Your love fill us. May that love overflow onto our brothers and sisters in Christ and show the world the meaning of being in the family of God. May our love for one another be used by You to cause those who do not yet know Jesus to be drawn to Him.

NO FEAR

In this way, love[G26] has been perfected among us, so that we may have confidence on the day of judgment; for in this world we are just like Him. There is no fear in love[G26], but perfect love[G26] drives out fear, because fear involves punishment. The one who fears has not been perfected in love[G26].

1 John 4:17-18

How are we just like Jesus? He paid the price for sin on the cross and that judgement is now behind Him. He paid that price in our place. Therefore, we do not need to fear the wrath of God. God sees us through the lens of Jesus's sacrifice and sees His righteousness covering us. Therefore, we can walk confidently through this world because of God's love for us.

> Just as judgment is passed for Him, so we are beyond the reach of condemnation. [55]

> **4:18 not been perfected in love.** God's love is perfect in itself, and it brings to us the sure promise of perfection as soon as we receive it (vv. 12, 17; 2:5). But because we are being made perfect in His

love over time (3:2), the remnants of fear may temporarily coexist with love. "Perfected love" from God "casts out fear" progressively rather than instantaneously. [56]

Proverbs 9:10 The fear of the Lord is the beginning of wisdom, And the knowledge of the Holy One is understanding.

Does 1 John 4:18 nullify Proverbs 9:10? NO! God's amazing love for us will intensify our reverence and awe of Him and inspire us to obedience. However, as His love is made mature in us, we will no longer fear judgment or punishment. Because Jesus paid the price for our sin (past, present, and future) on the cross, we have confidence to stand before God knowing He sees the righteousness of Jesus when He looks at us. We also need not fear anything that can happen to us in this world because we know our Father cares for us and is in control of every aspect of our lives (whether we feel like He is or not). Remember the first words of the angel to Mary and then to the shepherds, "Fear not!" Our Father knows we have a tendency toward fear and is lovingly helping us to overcome it. Casting out fear is a process, not a one-time event. God knows He created us from dust (Psalm 103:14), and is a patient, loving Father.

Are you fearful about judgment? If you belong to Jesus, you do not have to fear judgment any longer. Are you fearful about things happening in your life? Pray asking the Lord to remove that fear and replace it with confidence in His love for you. This may not happen immediately, but as you persist in reminding yourself of God's loving control, the fear will ebb away to be replaced with confidence in Christ.

Father, cast out any fear lingering in our emotions. We know in our minds and hearts that You love us and use everything for our good, but sometimes our feelings lag behind. Please increase our confidence, our complete trust in Your love.

HE FIRST LOVED US

We love[G25] *because He first loved*[G25] *us.*

1 John 4:19

All human love is preceded and generated by the love of God. [57]

The only reason we have the capacity to love is because God loved us first. Jesus loved us enough to go to the cross in our place. We love Him in return because of His love for us. After dying on the cross, Jesus rose again and is now interceding for us at the Father's throne. Everything Jesus did while on earth and now as He is back in Heaven, originated with His love for us. We do not have the ability to love sacrificially like our Lord on our own. Love does not originate with us but with the Lord. The only way we can love others and be a testimony to nonbelievers is to remain in the love of Jesus. We can only love the seemingly unlovable person because Jesus infuses us with His strength.

> *John 15:5 I am the vine and you are the branches. The one who remains in Me, and I in him, will bear much fruit. For apart from Me you can do nothing.*

Philippians 4:13 (AMPC) I have strength for all things in Christ Who empowers me [I am ready for anything and equal to anything through Him Who infuses inner strength into me; I am self-sufficient in Christ's sufficiency].

Take some time to reflect on God's amazing love and thank Him for enabling you to love Him and others. Perhaps listen to or sing along with "Amazing Love" performed by Phillips, Craig, and Dean. https://www.youtube.com/watch?v=Vf8vwxNzYAk

Father, contemplating Your love makes us want to sing praises to You. Thank You for teaching us how to love and empowering and enabling us to love.

LOVER OR LIAR?

If anyone says, "I love^{G25} God," but hates^{G3404} his broth-er^{G80}, he is a liar. For anyone who does not love^{G25} his brother, whom he has seen, cannot love^{G25} God, whom he has not seen. And we have this commandment from Him: Whoever loves^{G25} God must love^{G25} his brother^{G80} as well.

1 John 4:20-21

> G3404 *miséō* – With the acc. of person, usually implying active ill will in words and conduct, a persecuting spirit where it stands as opposite to agapáō, to love. [58]

> G80 *adelphós* - from G1 (as a connective particle) and δελφίς *delphýs* (the womb); a brother (literally or figuratively) . . . [59]

After reading several definitions for the Greek word translated here as "brother," we have come to the conclusion that this can mean a biological family member, a member of the same tribe or national origin, someone like a brother because of friendship, or a fellow member of the body of Christ. Biblical writers often used the masculine to refer to people in general, so we also believe this is true of females as well and could be "brother or sister." Basically, if we love God, we should not hate any person. We can hate the evil deeds but not the evil doers. We are to have Christ-like love that desires salvation for even those who have harmed us. Hatred is incompatible with the love (agapáō) that God places within us. If we say we love God but harbor hatred in our hearts, we are lying not only to others but to ourselves.

Do you continue to dwell on the hurt someone has caused you? Ask the Lord to help you to forgive. A moment of ill will toward someone may flit through us, but we should not nurture bad feelings. Bitterness and hatred harm the vessel that holds them. We are to be vessels filled to overflowing with the love of God, but first we may need to ask the Lord to wash away the hurt that tries to linger in us and enable us to forgive.

Father, we pray along with King David, "Create in me a clean heart, O God, and renew a right spirit within me" (Psalm 51:10). Remove any ill will we have toward a person before we let it fester into hatred. Fill us with Your love toward even those people who do harm. Enable us to obey Your command to love our enemies and pray for those who persecute us (Matthew 5:44). Help us to point them toward You and Your grace.

OVERCOMING THE WORLD

Everyone who believes that Jesus is the Christ has been born of God, and everyone who loves^{G25} the Father also loves^{G25} those born of Him. By this we know that we love^{G25} the children of God: when we love^{G25} God and keep His commandments. For this is the love^{G26} of God, that we keep His commandments. And His commandments are not burdensome, because everyone born of God overcomes the world. And this is the victory that has overcome the world: our faith.

1 John 5:1-4

Everyone who believes Jesus is the promised Messiah, the anointed One, and trusts in Him alone to make peace between them and God the Father, is now a member of the family of God. God drew us to have that faith—that trust in Jesus—by His lovingkindness. If we love Jesus, we will love the Father who sent Him and all those who are children of God by being born again— receiving God's gift of grace purchased on the cross by Jesus. What is the proof of our love for the Lord and our brothers and sisters in Christ? Keeping God's commandments. The commandments of God are relational. They involve right relationship with the Lord and with each other. Yes, Jesus died to purchase our redemption because we were incapable of keeping the commandments perfectly. However, now that His Holy Spirit indwells us, we are being made more and more like Christ. We are empowered to obey God. We are overcomers because His Holy Spirit enables us to say "no" to the world and "yes" to the Lord as He reveals His will and His ways through His word.

> *Titus 2:11-14 (NIV) For the grace of God has appeared that offers salvation to all people. It teaches us to say "No" to ungodliness and worldly passions, and to live self-controlled, upright and godly lives in this present age, while we wait for the blessed hope—the appearing of the glory of our great God and Savior, Jesus Christ, who gave himself for us to redeem us from all wickedness and to purify for himself a people that are his very own, eager to do what is good.*

Faith is the victory that overcomes the world, and faith is ours because God first loved us. Do you want to be an overcomer? Do you want to live victoriously even amid the struggles of life on this fallen earth? Love God. Love His children. Demonstrate this love of God by obeying His commandments. Put feet to your faith and live each day victoriously in His grace to the glory of God. Worship Opportunity (turn on closed captions: https://www.youtube.com/watch?v=DSNMQAVe7FE

Father, help us to be overcomers by exercising our faith and loving Your forever family. Help us to remember that Your Holy Spirit lives in us, and therefore, we are no longer slaves to sin but victors over it! Such love[G26] has no fear, because perfect love[G26] expels all fear. If we are afraid, it is for fear of punishment, and this shows that we have not fully experienced his perfect love.[G26]

1 John 4:18 (NLT)

PERFECT LOVE
(SONG LYRICS BY SUSIE HALE)

You are faithful,
every moment of every hour
of every single day.
You are near me, right beside me,
never leaving; You will never stray.

For Your love is perfect.
Your love is true.
No one else could ever love me
the way that You do!

So I will trust You, true submission,
complete surrender, I give to You my all.
Lead me; guide me.
Show me how I best can serve You.
I'm listening for Your call.

For Your love is perfect.
Your love is true.
No one else could ever love me
the way that You do!

LIVING IN LOVE

And now I urge you, dear lady—not as a new commandment to you, but one we have had from the beginning—that we love^G25 one another. And this is love^G26, that we walk according to His commandments. This is the very commandment you have heard from the beginning, that you must walk^G4043 in love^G26.

2 John 1:5-6

G4043 *peripatéō* – Figuratively, to live or pass one's life . . . implying manner or rule (60)

We do not know the identity of the "dear lady" to whom John wrote this letter. Some theorize it is a way to refer to the church, but most believe she was an actual woman with whom John was acquainted. He commends her for raising children who are walking in the truth (i.e. are believers). Then John reminds her of the importance of loving one another as Jesus had commanded His disciples when He walked with them on the earth. John is describing love as habitual and perpetual among the brothers and sisters in Christ. To "walk in" something is to live it daily. We are to walk in love. We are to *live* in love. Believers should be known for having a lifestyle of love. Love to the Christ-follower should be as natural as breathing. John MacArthur gives a good explanation of the Apostle John's definition of love:

> **2 John 1:6 This is love, that we walk according to His commandments**. John defines love, not as a sentiment or an emotion, but as obedience to God's commands (see notes on 1 John 5:2, 3). Those who are obedient to the truth as contained in God's commandments, the fundamentals of the faith (1 John 2:3–11), are identified as walking in love. Cf. John 14:15, 21; 15:10. [61]

If an outsider were to describe your lifestyle, would "love" be the first word they used? Are you consistently loving others as Jesus taught us? Does your obedience to God demonstrate your love for Him and others? Sometimes we need a reminder like the one John sent to the "dear lady" to whom his letter was addressed, a reminder to live in love.

Father, may our love for You and our brothers and sisters in Christ be evident to all. May our daily lives be characterized by Your love flowing through us by the power of the Holy Spirit within us. May we live in Your love.

MAY LOVE BE MULTIPLIED

*Jude, a servant of Jesus Christ and a brother of James,
To those who are called, loved^G25 by God the Father,
and kept in Jesus Christ: Mercy, peace, and love^G26 be
multiplied^G4129 to you.*

Jude 1:1-2

Jude identifies himself as a servant or bondslave of
Jesus Christ and a brother of James, the recognized
head of the church in Jerusalem. This would make him
a half-brother of Jesus. Jude does not claim that kinship
here. Perhaps that humility stems from the fact that he
did not believe Jesus to be the Messiah until after the
resurrection. Although not an Apostle, Jude's familial
relationship with James gives him the right to speak
with authority to believers. Mercy and peace were common Jewish greetings, but Christians added "love". Here
Jude prays that all three will be multiplied to his readers
who were brothers and sisters in Christ. Multiplied is
even more emphatic than added.

> G4129 *plēthýnō* - . . . meaning to abound
> to someone; 2 Peter 1:2, Jude 1:2 [62]

Jude was praying that mercy, peace, and love would be
abundant to believers. He was writing at a time when
Christians were being persecuted and many people were

turning from the true faith. False teachers were common. The believers needed God's mercy, peace, and love in order to stand firm in their faith. We need these same three things in abundance today because we face some of the same challenges.

Do an experiment this week. Greet a brother or sister in Christ with, "Mercy, peace, and love be multiplied to you" and note their reaction. Perhaps begin your email correspondence this way. Might we start a revival of encouragement by letting other believers know that this is our prayer for them? Would you like to be sincerely greeted in this way?

Father, let us know Your mercy, peace, and love in abundance. We know You give these freely, but sometimes we forget they are ours to embrace and share. Help us to assure other believers of Your mercy, peace, and love and use those traits in our lives to draw those who do not yet know Jesus into relationship with You.

STAND FIRM IN THE LOVE OF GOD

But you, beloved[G27], by building yourselves up in your most holy faith and praying in the Holy Spirit, keep[G5083] yourselves in the love[G26] of God as you await the mercy of our Lord Jesus Christ to bring you eternal life. . . Now to Him who is able to keep you from stumbling and to present you unblemished in His glorious presence, with great joy—to the only God our Savior be glory, majesty, dominion, and authority through Jesus Christ our Lord before all time, and now, and for all eternity.

Jude 1:20-21, 24-25

G5083 *tēréō* - cause one to persevere or stand firm in a thing. [(63)]

How are we as believers supposed to build ourselves up in the faith? Bible study, prayer, and "family-ship" help to keep us strong. "Keep" might be better translated "persevere" or "stand firm." If we are trying to keep ourselves in God's love in our own strength, we will fail. However, when we rely on the strength of the Lord, we will not fail because it is the Lord who enables us to stand firm.

Romans 14:4 Who are you to judge someone else's servant? To his own master he stands or falls. And he will stand, for the Lord is able to make him stand.

We are fortified, not because we are "super saints," but because we are surrendered to, sustained, and supported by the mighty hands of Jesus. We stand firm because we rest in His arms and trust Him to keep us in His love. However, when we are not "feeling" loved, we need to remind ourselves of God's unconditional, merciful, gracious love by studying His word, praying honestly to Him, and spending time with strong believers. Look back on your life or in your journal if you keep one and note the many times God's love has sustained you. In this way we can bring our feelings into alignment with the truth that we are held securely by Christ, and nothing can separate us from the love of God (Romans 8:35-39).

Father, remind us daily that we can stand firm in Your love because You hold us securely in Your hand (John 10:28-29) and no one can remove us from Your love. Help us to live boldly for You, confident of our place in Your forever family.

FIRST LOVE MUST BE FOREMOST

*I know your deeds, your labor, and your persever-
ance. I know that you cannot tolerate those who are
evil, and you have tested and exposed as liars those
who falsely claim to be apostles. Without growing
weary, you have persevered and endured many things
for the sake of My name. But I have this against you:
You have abandoned your first love^{G26}.*

Revelation 2:2-4

2:4 left your first love. To be a Christian is to love the Lord Jesus Christ (John
14:21, 23; 1 Cor. 16:22). But the Ephesians' passion and fervor for Christ had
become cold, mechanical orthodoxy.
Their doctrinal and moral purity, their
undiminished zeal for the truth, and their
disciplined service were no substitute for
the love for Christ they had forsaken. [64]

Good works that are not fueled by a fervent love for
Jesus are riddled with holes like a piece of Swiss
cheese. We can robotically do all the things we think a
Christian should do but have a stone-cold heart toward
God. Doing good out of obligation leaves the love of

Jesus behind. In other words, ritual without relationship has no real value. Even our "worship" can become "mouthing hymns and reading prayers" as a song from the musical "Real" described it. We can serve on the committees, feed the poor, attend and participate in all the Bible studies, cry out against injustice, etc. but no longer enjoy the intimate, loving relationship with God that Jesus died to give us!

If we find ourselves just "going through the motions," what should we do? First, examine whether we have truly surrendered to the Lord. If we are certain of our salvation, we may need to meditate on what Christ has done for us. If you are too busy to read the Bible and pray, you are too busy! Slow down from all the activity of modern Christianity and spend some quality time with the Christ, the Son of the living God, who loved us enough to leave Paradise knowing He was to die in our place, cruelly crucified. What greater love could there be?

> *John 15:13 Greater love has no one than this, that he lay down his life for his friends.*

Father, may we truly never forget what Christ did for us. Keep our hearts steadfast and firm in Your love. Let our love for You be the motivation for all that we do for others. Thank You for Your unfailing love!

CORRECTION IS CONFIRMATION OF HIS LOVE

Those I love^{G5368}, I rebuke and discipline. Therefore be
earnest and repent. Behold, I stand at the door and
knock. If anyone hears My voice and opens the door,
I will come in and dine with him, and he with Me.

Revelation 3:19-20

These verses are within the message to the church at Laodicea, the ones who were spiritually tepid, neither apathetically cold nor passionately hot, and the Lord said He would spit them out. Surprisingly, the word used for love in this passage is *philĕō*, a friendly, sibling affection, rather than agapăō which is a moral choice to love. To rebuke is to make someone aware of their faults; and to chasten is to discipline, teach, or punish. Jesus says that He points out the sin of those He loves, those who are His friends, and takes measures to correct them. The Lord's intent in showing us our sin (conviction) is to show us that we need to make an "about face" away from sin and make a beeline toward Jesus (repentance). Once we realize how far we are from Him, we will see that we need to trust His accomplished work on the cross and throw open the door for Him to walk through and take control of our lives. The Lord Jesus says he will sup (dine) with the one who invites Him in. This is more than just sharing a chicken fried steak and some sweet tea. This note from *The Complete Jewish Study Bible* explains what the Lord is truly saying:

> In Jewish culture meal sharing includes table fellowship, affection, intimacy and mutual confidence. In short, Yeshua is promising to be intimately and truly present with anyone who genuinely asks him. [66]

Notice that Jesus is not judging His friends when He rebukes them. Because He loves them, He is not willing to leave them in the sin that separates them from relationship with Him. One of the hardest things to do is to lovingly confront a friend who has strayed from the way Jesus would have them to go. However, it is one of the most loving things we can do on behalf of the "familyship" because it is for the sake of fellowship with the Lord and His fellowship with His bride. Sin impedes every kind of intimacy both with the Lord Jesus and within the Messianic community—all those who have trusted Jesus for salvation. Accountability is crucial to growth, and intimacy flourishes among those who love enough to gently rebuke each other.

The fruit of the Spirit is love. Genuine love cares enough to confront rather than bury that which separates a friend from the intense loving relationship with Jesus that restores vitality to life. When someone rebukes you, do you bristle? Remind yourself that they may be doing this most difficult task out of affection and for your protection. Their hope is to restore your intimacy with Jesus and deepen your friendship with them.

Father, help us to understand that correction indicates love. Thank You for loving us enough to convict us when we stray from Your path for us.

LOVE BEGINS AND ENDS WITH HIM

Because the Father first loved us,
We can love Him in return.
When we put our trust in Jesus,
From the Holy Spirit we'll learn
What it means to love sisters and brothers
Showing genuine concern.

Not only do we love believers—
Chosen children of our gracious Lord;
But we learn to love those who hate us,
To witness with kindness as well as words.
Our loving and kind actions
Set us apart from the rest of the herd.

We show them the Father loved us
And sent His Son to walk on earth,
To leave Heaven and all of its glory
To live humbly even from His birth.
Although His Father owns the cattle
on a thousand hills,
In this world Jesus had no net worth.

Yes, Jesus who was born in a stable
Was the Messiah the Bible foretold.
Jesus lived as the perfect God-man
and began His ministry at thirty years old.
He ruffled the feathers of the Pharisees
But preached His message fearless and bold.

He said the Kingdom of Heaven was near;
In fact, it was even at hand.
Along with this message of promise,
He healed people throughout the land.
He drove out demons from others,
And found Himself in much demand.

His miracles were demonstrations
Of His power, love, mercy, and grace;
But His love's greatest affirmation
Was He died on the cross in our place.
He paid the penalty for our sin
Dying cruelly in utter disgrace.

The most wonderful love you can ever know
Was made ours by His sacrifice.
He rose from the grave on the third day
Defeating death that we might have life.
He died even for the thief on the cross
Who would join Him in paradise.

If you will surrender to Jesus,
Trusting Him to have total control,
He will change your life completely
Take your brokenness and make you whole.
Someday you'll go to a place He's prepared
And in complete peace, you will stroll.

Once you receive His perfect love,
He'll perfect His love within you.
The Fruit of the Spirit will grow
becoming evident in all that you do.
You will spread His love to others
Because His love has made you new.

Yes, love begins and ends with God:
"We love because He first loved us."
In loving-kindness, He drew us to Jesus
And enabled us to trust.
Since we are now Christ-followers,
Loving God and others is a must.

JEWELS OF SALVATION

❖ *Romans 3:22-24 And this righteousness from God comes through faith in Jesus Christ to all who believe. There is no distinction, **for all have sinned and fall short of the glory of God**, and are justified freely by His grace through the redemption that is in Christ Jesus.*

Everyone on earth has sinned. Sin is both doing things that go against what God tells us to do in the Bible and failing to do the good things He instructs us to do. This failure brings the wrath of God on us, and Jesus is the **only way** to make peace with God. John 14:6 "Jesus answered, "I am the way and the truth and the life. No one comes to the Father except through Me.""

❖ *Romans 6:20-23 For when you were slaves to sin, you were free of obligation to righteousness. What fruit did you reap at that time from the things of which you are now ashamed? The outcome of those things is death. But now that you have been set free from sin and have become slaves to God, the fruit you reap leads to holiness, and the outcome is eternal life. **For the wages of sin is death, but the gift of God is eternal life in Christ Jesus our Lord.***

The punishment for sin is death. The official term is "substitutionary atonement" which simply means you were sentenced to the death penalty, but Jesus volunteered to die on the cross in your place in order for you to be set free. Jesus died a painful death to redeem you from slavery to sin and spare you from the wrath of the righteous, Holy God.

❖ *Romans 5:6-8 For at just the right time, while we were still powerless, Christ died for the ungodly. Very rarely will anyone die for a righteous man, though for a good man someone might possibly dare to die.* **But God proves His love for us in this: While we were still sinners, Christ died for us.**

Jesus died while we were still sinners. "For God so loved the world that **He gave His one and only Son**, that everyone who believes in Him shall not perish but have eternal life."

❖ *Romans 10:8-10 But what does it say? "The word is near you; it is in your mouth and in your heart," that is, the word of faith we are proclaiming: that* **if you confess with your mouth, "Jesus is Lord," and believe in your heart that God raised Him from the dead, you will be saved.** *For with your heart you believe and are justified, and with your mouth you confess and are saved.*

1 Corinthians 15:3-4 "For what I received I passed on to you as of first importance: that Christ died for our sins according to the Scriptures, that He was buried, that He was raised on the third day according to the Scriptures . . ." If you believe that Jesus is the Son of God who died for you and was raised to life, then trust in, rely on, Him to save you from the wrath of God, you can belong to Jesus.

❖ *Romans 10:11-13 It is just as the Scripture says: "Anyone who believes in Him will never be put to shame." For there is no difference between Jew and Greek: The same Lord is Lord of all, and gives richly to all who call on Him, for,* ***"Everyone who calls on the name of the Lord will be saved."***

How do you become a member of the family of God? Pray—talk to God admitting that you cannot be good enough, obey all His commands. Tell Him you trust that Jesus died on the cross to save you from slavery to sin and the wrath of God. Ask God to place His Holy Spirit in you and change you from the inside out. Thank Him for giving you life in His presence forever.

BELIEVER'S BENEFITS

The obvious benefit of trusting in Jesus, the Son of God who died for you and was raised from the grave to return to the right hand of His Father, and surrendering your life to him, is that instead of spending eternity separated from God and all that is good you will live in His presence in complete peace and joy. However, those who become the Lord's children by relying on Jesus gain many other things in this current life on earth. Here are a few:

❖**Lord, we thank you for freeing us from slavery to sin and providing a way to flee temptation!** *Romans 6:6 "We know that our old self was crucified with Him so that the body of sin might be rendered powerless, that **we should no longer be slaves to sin."** This does not mean that a believer will never sin again. It means he/she now has a choice to tap into the Holy Spirit's power to resist the urge to give in to temptation. "No temptation has seized you except what is common to man. And God is faithful; He will not let you be tempted beyond what you can bear. But **when you are tempted, He will also provide an escape,** so that you can stand up under it" (1 Corinthians 10:13).*

❖**Lord, thank You that nothing can separate us from Your love!** *"For I am convinced that neither death nor life, neither angels nor principalities, neither the present nor the future, nor any powers, neither height nor depth, nor anything else in all creation, will* *be able to separate us from the love of God that is in Christ Jesus our Lord" (Romans 8:38-39).*

❖**Lord, thank You that our salvation is secure and cannot be lost!** *John 10:27-29 "My sheep listen to My voice; I know them, and they follow Me. I give them eternal life, and they will never perish.* **No one can snatch them out of My hand.** *My Father who has given them to Me is greater than all. No one can snatch them out of My Father's hand."*

❖**Lord thank you for empowering us to do whatever You call us to do!** *Philippians 4:13 (AMP) "I can do all things [which He has called me to do] through Him who strengthens and empowers me [to fulfill His purpose—I am self-sufficient in Christ's sufficiency; I am ready for anything and equal to anything* **through Him who infuses me with inner strength and confident peace.]**

❖**Lord, thank You for giving us brothers and sisters all over the world!** *"Respect everyone, and love the* **family of believers.***" 1 Peter 2:17a (NLT).*

DICTIONARY OF "SUSANISMS"

Bed-found –   This is preferred over "bed-bound" because Susan is not chained to her bed, but these days it is usually where Susan is found.

CareGIVER – Caregivers take care of people. Caretakers maintain houses, buildings, or cemeteries! Susie is my caregiver, and I am hers!

Familyship – The family of God. We prefer "familyship" over "fellowship" because, obviously, we are not all fellows.

Framily – Friends who have become family because of our mutual love for Jesus, our brothers and sisters in Christ which may include our biological family as well.

Full-weight -   Susan is not "dead weight" when we lift her because she is very much alive! We are simply bearing her full weight because she cannot assist us.

Remnants – Susan does not call her shortened legs "stumps," because stumps are something you put in a woodchipper. Her legs are "remnants" because Jesus saves and returns for the remnant.

Tater – This is Susan's nickname or job description for Susie. It is short for facilitator because Susie facilitates many things for her.

Finally, PLEASE do not refer to Susan as an invalid. She is not IN-valid. Here is her description of herself:

> ***I am uniquely fit for His service—***
> ***a divinely designed presentation!***

NOTES

1. Baker, Warren and Carpenter, Eugene, eds., *The Complete Word Study Dictionary: Old Testament,* H157, H160, H2617.

2. Zodhiates, Spiros, ed., *The Complete Word Study Dictionary: New Testament,* G25, G26, G27, G5360, G5368, G5387.

3. Swindoll, Charles R., *Swindoll's Living Insights New Testament Commentary: Matthew 1-15,* pp. 204 & 206.

4. Strong, James, *The New Strong's Exhaustive Concordance of the Bible,* G4413.

5. Zodhiates, G25.

6. Zodhiates, G5368.

7. MacArthur, John, *NKJV MacArthur Study Bible, 2nd Edition,* note on Romans 5:5.

8. Zodhiates, G18.

9. Webster, Noah, *The American Dictionary of the English Language, 1828.* Definition of "dissimulation."

10. Strong, G505.

11. Zodhiates, G5387.

12. Zodhiates, G5360.

13. Zodhiates, G3114.

14. Zodhiates, G5541.

15. Zodhiates, G2206.

16. Oxford Dictionary at https://languages.oup.com/ , definition of "envy."

17. Zodhiates, G4068.

18. Zodhiates, G5448.

19. Zodhiates, G809.

20. Zodhiates, G2212.

21. Zodhiates, G3947.

22. Zodhiates, G3049.

23. Zodhiates, G5463

24. Zodhiates, G93

25. Zodhiates, G4796

26. Zodhiates, G225

27. Zodhiates, G4722

28. Zodhiates, G4100

29. Zodhiates, G1679

30. Zodhiates, G5278

31. Jamieson, Robert, A. R. Fausset and David Brown, *A Commentary, Critical, Practical, and Explanatory on the Old and New Testaments –* Commentary on 1 Corinthians 13:7 "hope".

32. Zodhiates, G1601.

33. Strong, G1601.

34. Zodhiates, G4102.

35. Webster, definition of faith.

36. Zodhiates, G1680.

37. Webster, definition of hope.

38. Zodhiates, G26,

39. Webster, definition of love.

40. Zodhiates, G27.

41. MacArthur, note on Philippians 1:9 as quoted at www.biblegateway.com.

42. MacArthur, note on Philippians 2:2-3

43. Encyclopedia Britannica, quoted at https://www.britannica.com/, definition of Sari.

44. Strong, G4052.

45. Vines, Jerry, *Vines' Expository Bible Notes,* note on 1 Thessalonians 3:12 found at www.biblegateway.com

46. Thayer, Joseph, *Thayer's Greek-English Lexicon of the New Testament,* G1343.

47. Zodhiates, G3784.

48. MacArthur, note on 1 John 3:16.

49. Zodhiates, G25.

50. Zodhiates, G27.

51. Zodhiates, G3784.

52. MacArthur, note on 1 John 4:11.

53. Zodhiates, G5048.

54. Wiersbe, Warren, *NKJV Wiersbe Study Bible,* note on 1 John 4:16b.

55. MacDonald, William, *Believer's Bible Commentary,* note on 1 John 4:17-18.

56. Sproul, R. C. *ESV Reformation Study Bible,* note on 1 John 4:18.

57. Vincent, Marvin R., *Word Studies in the New Testament, Volume 2: The Writings of John,*

58. Zodhiates, G3404.

59. Strong, G80.

60. Zodhiates, G4043.

61. MacArthur, notes on 2 John 1:6

62. Zodhiates, G4129.

63. Thayer, G5083.

64. MacArthur, note on Revelation 2:4.

65. Wiersbe, note on Revelation 2:19.

66. Rubin, Rabbi Barry, *The Complete Jewish Study Bible,* note on Revelation 3:20.

BIBLIOGRAPHY

Baker, Warren and Carpenter, Eugene, eds., *The Complete Word Study Dictionary: Old Testament*, (Chattanooga, TN: AMG Publishers, 2003).

MacDonald, William, *Believer's Bible Commentary,* (Thomas Nelson, 2016).

Encyclopedia Britannica, quoted at
https://www.britannica.com/

*A Commentary, Critical, Practical, and Explanatory on the Old and New Testaments, (*Robert Jamieson, A. R. Fausset and David Brown, 1882).

MacArthur, John, *NKJV Macarthur Study Bible, 2nd Edition,* (Thomas Nelson, 1997, 2006, 2019), as quoted on www.biblegateway.com

Oxford Dictionary at https://languages.oup.com/

Rubin, Rabbi Barry, *The Complete Jewish Study Bible,* (Hendrickson Publishers, 2016).

Sproul, R. C. *ESV Reformation Study Bible*, (Reformation Trust Publishing of Ligonier Ministries, 2021).

Strong, James, *The New Strong's Exhaustive Concor-*

dance of the Bible, (Thomas Nelson, 2009).

Swindoll, Charles R., *Swindoll's Living Insights New Testament Commentary: Matthew 1-15*, (Carol Stream, Illinois, Tyndale House Publishers, 2020).

Thayer, Joseph, *Thayer's Greek-English Lexicon of the New Testament,* (Hendrickson Publishers, 1996).

Vincent, Marvin R., *Word Studies in the New Testament, Volume 2: The Writings of John* (MacDonald Publishing, 1985)

Vines, Jerry, *Vines' Expository Bible Notes,* (Thomas Nelson, 2020), as quoted at www.biblegateway.com.

Webster, Noah, *The American Dictionary of the English Language, 1828.* as found at https://webstersdictionary1828.com/

Wiersbe, Warren, *NKJV Wiersbe Study Bible,* (Thomas Nelson, 2021).

Zodhiates, Spiros, ed., *The Complete Word Study Dictionary: New Testament* (Chattanooga, TN: AMG Publishers, 2000).

ABOUT THE AUTHORS

SUSAN SLADE is an ordained minister (Fellowship of Churches and Christian Ministries, now a part of Kerygma Ventures). She earned a BA in English Bible with minors in Pastoral Counseling and Modern Hebrew and a MA in Biblical Literature from Oral Roberts University in Tulsa, Oklahoma. She is the founder and president of Precious Jewels Ministries, Inc., a 501(c)3. She was a guest of "Life Today" with James Robinson. The Lord enables Susan to overcome Cerebral Palsy to serve Him with joy. She previously wrote a devotional book titled A Life's Symphony of Joy and co-authored a year-long devotional titled Let Him In and two shorter books titled Thirty Days of Thanksgiving Praise, and From Prophecy to Perfection: A Treasury of Christmas Devotions with her partner in ministry Susie Hale.

KAREN SUE HALE (SUSIE) has a BA in Music Education and a M.Ed. with a focus on language arts and serves as Vice President and Secretary of Precious Jewels Ministries. In addition to co-authoring books with Susan, she previously had two articles published in "Purposeful Singleness Monthly" and one published on "Christian Women Today," a webzine. Susie taught eleven years at Glenview Christian School in Ft. Worth, Texas and served as curriculum coordinator there. Susie is Susan's "facilitator" assisting with daily living and more importantly Bible study, making use of her language arts and computer skills.

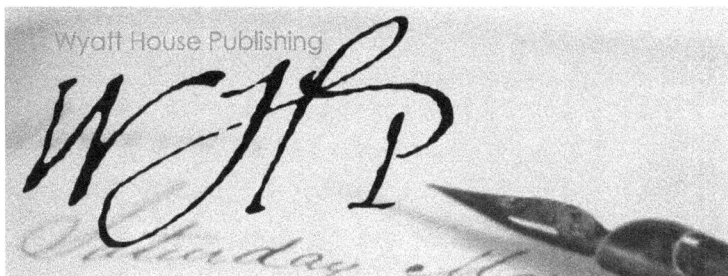

www.ingramcontent.com/pod-product-compliance
Lightning Source LLC
Chambersburg PA
CBHW021504090426

42739CB00007B/460

*9 7 8 1 9 5 4 7 9 8 1 6 8 *